The
Six-Legged
Dog

The
Six-Legged
Dog

MATTEI AND *ENI*—A STUDY IN POWER

by Dow Votaw

PUBLICATIONS OF THE INSTITUTE OF BUSINESS AND ECONOMIC RESEARCH
UNIVERSITY OF CALIFORNIA

UNIVERSITY OF CALIFORNIA PRESS
BERKELEY AND LOS ANGELES   1964

University of California Press
Berkeley and Los Angeles, California

Cambridge University Press
London, England

© 1964 by The Regents of the University of California

Library of Congress Catalog Card Number 64-18648

to mairn

Preface

There is no need to explain why this book was written. Enrico Mattei and his Ente Nazionale Idrocarburi are and will continue to be fascinating subjects of economic, legal, political, sociological, and historical research. The surface has been scratched only slightly. Another dimension was added to the ENI story by Mattei's tragic death in October, 1962, but it is still too soon to be able to understand or to describe its scope. The primary concern of this book is with ENI under Mattei, and only brief attention is given to the effect of his death.

The long hiatus following the Italian elections in the spring of 1963, which apparently came to an end with the formation of the Moro cabinet in November, 1963, has given Mattei's successors an opportunity to establish their own imprint upon the Ente and upon the Italian scene before a stable government could bring its policies to bear upon ENI and upon the other government-owned Italian companies. Only time now can tell how the issues raised in this book will be dealt with by the coalition cabinet which has finally "opened to the left" to admit the Nenni Socialists.

I wish to express my deep appreciation to the ENI officers and employees, in Rome, Milan, and elsewhere in Italy, who gave so willingly of their time and so frankly of their views. Mr. Mattei was one to whom appreciation would in particular be due, were he still with us. He was extremely coöperative and raised no barriers whatever to the preparation of a manuscript which he must have known would include some sharp criticisms of him and of his policies. He was a very interesting man, and I am glad that I had a chance to know him.

The Institute of Business and Economic Research, University of California, supported me with travel money and editorial services, without which this book would never have materialized. I wish to acknowledge also the help of the office staff in the School of Business Administration.

Dow Votaw

Berkeley, California

Contents

CHAPTER I

The Setting

In English, "National Hydrocarbon Agency" sounds as though it might be an obscure federal bureau under the Department of Commerce charged with investigating working conditions in the kerosene industry. But in Italian, "Ente Nazionale Idrocarburi" (ENI) is at once a major political issue, a matter of national pride, a thorn in the side of the international petroleum industry, and the best hope for solution of Italy's economic ills; its initials seem to "scorch any lips that utter them," [1] and it is the repository of tremendous political, social, and economic power.

ENI is the center of an intense ideological, political, and economic dispute which has gripped Italy for years, and which is being forced to a head as a result of the nationalization of the entire Italian electric power industry [2] under the control of the newly created [3] "Ente per l'Energia Elettrica" (ENEL).

It would be very difficult today to find an Italian who was not either a violent opponent of ENI or a rabid defender—or afraid to be identified with either side. ENI wears both halo and horns, and the dispute has been aptly denominated as "theological." [4] The very ardor with which the dispute has been carried on has tended to conceal the real issues and drag the arguments off into irrelevancies.

But the power drama of ENI would probably never have been staged had it not been for its author, producer, and star, Enrico Mattei. This man, government employee and civil servant who headed the great Ente, has been called Italy's "grey eminence," "the most powerful man in Italy," and "minister without portfolio." He has been compared with Hitler and Castro, Rockefeller and

Garibaldi, Napoleon and Cromwell, and with the "condottieri."
Italy's "modern miracle" has been credited to his genius; it has
also been said that most of Italy's problems could have been
solved by putting Mattei in prison.

In the brief period since 1953 when ENI was created by the
Italian Parliament as a successor to the older AGIP (Azienda
Generale Italiana Petroli) in the hydrocarbon field, Italy's fright-
ening shortage of sources of energy has been reversed so spectacu-
larly that it now appears that Italy can export gasoline and other
petroleum products in substantial quantities, market petroleum
products in a dozen lands outside Italy, and even build a pipeline
to supply refineries in Switzerland, Germany, and Austria.
Whether these results have been firmly established, how they have
come about—whether because of ENI and Mattei, and whether
they really have any long-run significance are issues to be considered in this essay, along with an examination of the economic
and political problems lying hidden in this powerful new form of
international society. Mattei's six-legged dog is ENI, a phenomenon in power.

Much has been written in recent years about the large, privately
owned, international corporations—about their autonomy in the
conduct of what amounts to quasi-public or even public activities,
and about their power. We shall see in this study strong parallels
between the issues raised by the private, quasi-public corporations
and public, quasi-private corporations such as ENI. One basic
similarity is that both raise the question of how far and in what
ways either may be permitted to make decisions affecting the
position of the national government. For example, does the fact
that ENI is a public corporation and Standard Oil Company of
New Jersey a private corporation make any real difference in the
"foreign policy" they shape for their respective governments in
the Middle East? In a very real sense Italy's elected government
has had much less influence over its own agency, ENI, than the
government of the United States has over Standard Oil Company
of New Jersey, a private corporation.

Those who have some familiarity with Italy may ask justifiably
why, out of the vast conglomeration of public companies in that

country, ENI has made such an impression. Another public
corporation in the industrial sector of the economy, IRI (Istituto
per la Ricostruzione Industriale), is much older [5] than ENI and
more than twice as large, but is almost unknown outside Italy,
and inside Italy has never been the center of widespread controversy, credited with "miracles," or charged with gross calumny.
Many Italians asked me why I bothered with ENI when IRI was
a much more interesting subject. The explanation of this paradox
was Mattei. IRI's executives, whose names would hardly be recognized outside the company, preside over a loose conglomeration
of almost independent subsidiaries and affiliates.[6] Mattei, from the
very beginning, identified ENI with himself and himself with
Italy. Italians look on IRI as a company but on ENI as Mattei.
The result has been a tightly and personally controlled organization on the economic level, a unitary personification on the political level, and more than a modicum of nationalistic pride on all
levels. Even Mattei's severest detractors found themselves unable
to overcome the influence of this tripartite arrangement, and it
was for Mattei a tremendous source of power. "This history of
ENI must be the biography of Mattei." [7]

There is not much doubt, economically speaking and in the
short run, that ENI and Mattei have been good for Italy. The
natural gas in the Po Valley, and now elsewhere in Italy, provided
badly needed energy at a most opportune time. Industrial ventures at Ravenna, Bari, Gela, Florence, and at many other places
have given new life to a wide variety of industries and communi-
ties. It can be said with certainty that the performance of ENI
has helped to restore the confidence of Italians in their ability
to hold their own in domestic and foreign economic affairs, to
discover and develop natural resources both at home and abroad,
and to compete effectively for international markets with even the
best of the well-established foreign companies. But the genuine
enthusiasm created by real and apparent success in some sectors
obscured the lack of success in others, the high price paid for
short-run gains in some areas, and the very thin economic thread
from which hangs the future of the Ente. Most important, perhaps, the aura of success concealed the vast personal power which

Mattei wielded. Thus, ENI's accomplishments, and the justified enthusiasm they engender, mask many serious problems. This is not to imply that success and its appreciation are inherently dangerous; it is to say that in Italy, as circumstances exist there in the early 1960's, the achievements of Mattei and ENI have tended to direct attention away from many of the political, social, and economic ramifications of their activities.

This paradoxical result is not entirely fortuitous. Mattei's skill in the public relations and propaganda techniques made it possible for him to create the kind of public image of himself and of his company that he desired. His own daily newspaper, *Il Giorno*, became an influential journal of national circulation, the second largest in Italy, with a policy which has been based on the further-ance of Mattei's personal objectives. Every criticism of ENI or of Mattei met with barrages of vituperation, countercharges, false and misleading information, and attacks *ad hominem*. Every re-sponse to Mattei's own attacks on private business or another oil company met with the same treatment.[8] Mattei had the support of the far-left press, and his antiprivate business and anti-American vituperation got extensive play or supporting blasts from *L'Unità* and other Communist newspapers. It must be said, however, that Mattei also courted the extreme right, attracting that portion of the political rainbow by means of nationalistic pronouncements; but the support from the left was vastly more important in terms of political power and of widespread public backing.

Herein lies, I believe, the most serious long-run issue created by Mattei and his Ente. Both of them became so thoroughly identi-fied with political positions, policies and polemics, that any criticism, suggestion, or recommendation directed at ENI or its president had to be prepared to run the gauntlet of vitriolic attack by extremist politicians and press, including *Il Giorno*. All of this would be interesting enough had Mattei been an elected official or a private business tycoon, but it is nothing short of astonishing when we remind ourselves that Mattei was only an appointed civil servant.

Enrico Mattei died tragically on October 27, 1962, at the age of 56, in an airplane crash south of Milan. It seems highly unlikely that the government in power could have won a showdown with Mattei if the occasion for challenge had arisen. Such a challenge did not occur before his death, but there were so many areas of potential conflict that a showdown probably could not have been avoided for many more years. For example, Italy is and has been one of the staunchest and most active supporters of NATO and of the West, yet in 1962–63 ENI bought up to 38 per cent of its crude oil needs from the Soviet Union, in exchange for such strategic materials as steel pipe [9] and synthetic rubber, making Italy by far the largest purchaser of Soviet oil outside the Iron Curtain. If the government had attempted to impose contrary policies on Mattei during these negotiations, it seems very doubtful now that it could have prevailed. The political involvement of ENI under Mattei had become so thorough and its political stands so strong and uncompromising that the prospects of resolving even small differences between Mattei and the government without major political upheaval were not very good. Mattei's death postponed the showdown, perhaps permanently, but the government is now faced with the decision as to the kind of leadership ENI and other nationalized industries should have. It is not likely, however, that even a decision in favor of strong, independent leadership will soon produce another Mattei. This issue is considered in greater detail in Chapter 6.

In addition to extensive involvement in noneconomic activities, Mattei took ENI far outside the scope of the project as described in the enabling statute of 1953 and expanded the range of ENI's influence far beyond the meaning of the term "hydrocarbons." The recent acquisition of a woolen knitting mill (Lanerossi) made it clear that leaving the determination of the scope of the ENI statute to Mattei removed all obvious boundaries to his activities. Furthermore, although Mattei professed to be an antimonopolist and wooed the far left with antimonopolist harangues, his conduct was as monopolistic and monopoly-minded as anything to be seen during the heyday of America's capitalist "robber barons."

Mattei aimed at monopoly in everything he did. He drove the competition out of the Po Valley. He was a major factor in the passage of the Oil Law of 1957 [10] through which, to all practical purposes, he drove all competition in search and production from the mainland of Italy. He began a campaign in 1961, with the help of the Communists, to do the same in Sicily. His independent arrangement with Morocco for building a refinery in that country included exclusive rights to import oil. "Socialist robber baron" accurately describes Enrico Mattei, President of ENI 1953–1962 and a paradox in power. His prototypes were the traditional "robber barons," acquisitive primarily of wealth, whereas Mattei was acquisitive primarily of power.

A psychiatrist might tell us the significance of Mattei's having chosen a fire-breathing, six-legged dog as the symbol of his new petroleum power. Whatever the reasons for his choice, the dog with the incendiary breath and two more legs than dogs are accustomed to having became especially appropriate to this hotly controversial man who had far more effect on Italy and on the world than one could reasonably expect of an Italian civil servant.

In the pages to follow, we shall trace the development of the unusual power phenomenon created by Mattei and then take a closer look at some of the important details of ENI's position in the economic, political, and social scene in present-day Italy. These measures must be taken before we can make a direct approach to the power aspects of the situation. Chapter 2 is a short history of ENI. Chapters 3 and 4 elaborate on some of the manifestations and apparatus of Mattei's power. In Chapter 5 a modern concept of power is developed and applied to Mattei and ENI; it will be discovered here that observable phenomena conform rather closely to modern power theory and that a useful case study in power can be built on the ENI experience. Certain conclusions are drawn in Chapter 6 with regard to power situations in general and with regard to modern public corporations in particular.

The lessons to be learned from ENI and Mattei may be helpful in providing us with a better understanding of power in a social context and in giving us a new appreciation of a "third form" of economic and political organization with which we can influence our world-wide struggle with the problems of industrial society and of the emerging nations.

CHAPTER 2

Penury
to Power

One of the factors that prevented Italy from accompanying the rest of Europe into a modern industrial society was the absence of cheap and plentiful sources of energy. The coal that fueled the Industrial Revolution in England, France, and Germany was in short supply in Italy and of poor quality. For generations Italy has had to import coal from abroad, primarily from England and the United States, at a cost that strapped Italy's foreign exchange and restricted industrial expansion. Hydroelectric sites not fully developed were heavily concentrated in the north and could not supply Italy's needs for energy. The geological signs of petroleum deposits were favorable in many parts of Italy and Sicily, but nothing more than dribbles of natural gas and liquid petroleum had ever been discovered or developed until the late 1940's. Italy imported almost all of its petroleum needs, again reducing foreign exchange and limiting expansion.[1] Although most of the other countries became twentieth-century industrial economies, Italy made only fitful, uncoördinated, and widely isolated starts in that direction.

Nobody was more aware than the Italians of the millstone which the shortage of energy placed around their necks. Even the Fascists, in spite of their preoccupation with mythical nonsense, originally saw the energy shortage as the core of the problem of making Italy a world power, but never succeeded in doing anything of lasting importance about it. Mussolini's paranoia finally convinced him and his followers that Italy was a great world power even without adequate supplies of energy. Hitler encouraged Mussolini's delusions during the 1930's for his own ends but paid history's price in later years when Mussolini began to base his actions on these same delusions. In their own inimitable and unbelievable fashion, the Fascists solved the energy problem by pretending it was not there.

The Fascists were not totally inactive in the energy field, though their efforts in this direction came largely to nought. By the Law of April 3, 1926,[2] Mussolini's government created a public corporation, the Azienda Generale Italiana Petroli (AGIP), primarily for the purpose of seeking out petroleum deposits in Italy but also for the broader purpose of pursuing solutions to the shortage of petroleum energy. Though making no great advances in Italy, AGIP did acquire substantial interests in oil fields and petroleum operations outside of Italy. For a short time after 1931, AGIP even had a controlling interest in the British Oil Development Company, with large concession rights in Iraq west of the Tigris, and for many years owned shares in Rumanian fields and in other areas. But, as with so many of his activities during his almost twenty-five years in power, Mussolini's delusions, abrupt changes of policy, and blustering and threatening postures spoiled his chances. "Mare nostrum" alienated those who controlled the access to some of Italy's potential sources of oil; other sources were sold or traded in order to obtain short-run advantages in arenas not involving petroleum; and what was left was often unproductive or easily cut off in case of war.

AGIP spent huge sums of money in its search for oil and gas in Italy but was handicapped by inefficiency, political meddling, lack of genuine government encouragement and support, and simple bad luck. AGIP became the dumping ground for worn-out political hacks and superannuated civil servants, a haven for the still all-too-common nomad of Italian society: the unproductive employee who is never discharged but who bounces around from office to office and agency to agency until he reaches the job from which there is no return. This was unfortunate for Italy's energy problems. When World War II ended, AGIP was ordered liquidated and its entire assets were put up for sale for sixty million lire, but there were no takers. It was at this low point, strangely enough, that Italy's modern petroleum history began.

Mattei

The Italian government made a genuine effort at the end of the war to populate its responsible offices and agencies with people who carried a minimum of fascist taint. Because almost everyone had been touched to some degree, the selection was a matter of picking those with the least taint rather than those with none. During the early postwar period, a great deal of deliberate attention was devoted to the task of distributing commissionerships, directorships, jobs as chiefs of police and the presidencies and vice-presidencies of public companies. Partisan leaders and university professors came in for a large share of these positions.[3] Among those clearly deserving of recognition was Enrico Mattei, a successful businessman, an influential and devoted lay Catholic, and one of the few non-Communist Partisan leaders. The Committee of National Liberation made Mattei Northern Commissioner for AGIP in 1945, and shortly thereafter Managing Director. His instructions were to carry out the liquidation of AGIP.

Mattei was born in Acqualagna in The Marches to a family of humble Abruzzese origin, though, at the time of Enrico's birth in 1906, his father was an officer in the *carabinieri*. The father left this position in 1919 and moved with his family of five children to Matelica. Enrico had to leave school at the age of fifteen and go to work. After a brief period as a painter, he obtained a job as errand boy in a tannery, and it was here that Mattei's unusual drive became apparent. In the space of three years, he is reputed to have risen to the post of manager of the tannery, which had over 150 employees. Mattei was not content to spend his life in the provinces and so quit this job. At the age of twenty-three he went to Milan, where he became a salesman of German industrial equipment. He soon was borrowing money (an art at which in later years he was to demonstrate real virtuosity as president of ENI) for the purpose of setting up his own chemical business. He was successful on a modest scale, and his future again appeared to be established, but this time the war and the Italian defeat intervened. With his usual complete absorption in whatever he had to do, Mattei joined the Resistance and became an outstanding organizer of Partisan brigades.[4] He had the usual collection of adventures, arrests, escapes, and other opportunities to show bravery—all now probably somewhat embroidered by time and by his supporters—but he was rewarded for his work with the Gold Medal of the Resistance, the American Silver Star, and election to Parliament. Again his future in business or politics seemed clear and secure, but he accepted the rather lowly post of Commissioner of AGIP.

Perhaps Mattei looked upon the job as simply an interlude, temporary in duration, before going back to his chemical business or on to something bigger. He probably could have become police chief of Milan or a member of the Consiglio of Montecatini, but instead he joined AGIP. It would not be very difficult to believe that he saw an opportunity in the defunct AGIP and a challenge in the order to liquidate its obsolete and deteriorated equipment. It can be agreed, however, that, whether as police chief, a member of the Consiglio, or as sewer commissioner, Mattei would have been heard from and would soon have become the same dynamic, aggressive, and controversial figure that he actually became through AGIP and ENI. A remote possibility is that Mattei saw in AGIP a possible solution to Italy's acute shortage of energy.

METHANE AND MONOPOLY

Fate, vision, opportunity, or whatever, Mattei became commissioner and then managing director of AGIP and proceeded to ignore the government's instructions to liquidate.[5] Whether these were his intentions when he took the job Mattei never said, but there is evidence to support the view that some of the young technicians working for AGIP, especially a geophysicist named Rocco, persuaded Mattei very soon that they could find substantial amounts of oil and gas in the Po Valley if he would ignore the liquidation orders for a few months longer. He did ignore his orders, in spite of repeated demands that they be carried out, and gave instructions to drill for oil and gas. Where the necessary funds came from is not known,[6] but it is known that he drilled large numbers of wells. He has been accused, like Joan of Arc and Charles de Gaulle, of listening to inner voices and to no others. Everyone admits that in Mattei's case these advisers were remarkably good. There is no way now to determine what the odds were on this gamble, but, luck or vision, Mattei was successful here. Gas in good quantities was found in 1946, and in large quantities in 1949. As an illustration of the ancient and wise observation that "most luck is made not had," one of Mattei's major strikes came through in the presence of Finance Minister Vanoni (who afterwards became one of Mattei's strongest supporters) and a large group of invited newspapermen and photographers. This strike was made at Cortemaggiore, which name became the basis for an AGIP trade name and slogan: SUPER-CORTEMAGGIORE, LA POTENTE BENZINA ITALIANA. Mattei was on his way.

The Po Controversy

One is inclined to wonder what changes there would have been in the course of history had Mussolini found the Po Valley methane back in the 1930's. Had he overcome his bias against foreigners, especially Americans, and made use of American money and skill in his search for hydrocarbons, AGIP probably would have found the Po fields many years before Mattei appeared on the scene. Jingoism was not invented by Mussolini; it runs deep through Italian history. Foreign bids for railroad electrification were turned down by the government in 1897 because it was unwilling to allow foreign companies to gain participation in Italian resources, and there were even loud protests against foreign generosity in helping to rebuild the Campanile of St. Mark's in Venice after it collapsed in 1902. Prime Minister Francesco Nitti was roundly condemned for permitting American capital to participate in the building of large hydroelectric plants in Calabria and Sardinia prior to World War I.

Mattei was too wise to permit jingoist feelings to interfere with his obtaining the best technical assistance, wherever it might be found. In spite of his bitter attacks on the American oil companies, Mattei sought their partnership in operating refineries, employed their technicians and techniques in his own search for oil, hired an American consulting firm to help him improve the organization of ENI, copied American service stations and motels, and in a dozen other ways indicated that he was not going to permit bitterness to interfere with good sense.

As soon as the Cortemaggiore and other large strikes made it clear that the Po Valley deposits were large and valuable, the Ministry of Industry and Commerce was flooded with applications from oil companies of many nations, seeking concession rights in the area. Power acquisitive Mattei wanted exclusive control for himself. Most of the applicants also sought a change in the Italian oil laws which permitted almost anyone to get authorization to search for oil, but did not state expressly that discovery under such authorization carried with it the right to exploit the findings. Perhaps the right to exploit was implicit in the right to search, but the oil companies, especially some of the large American ones, were not satisfied with this. Their aggressive tactics in connection with applications for concessions and with attempts to change the law played into Mattei's hands. Although the De Gasperi government was deeply committed to a competitive free enterprise system, Mattei's stage-managing of his battle for monopoly rights was so skillful and imaginative [7] that he eventually got what he wanted. The battle was hard fought and lasted until the Law of February 10, 1953, brought ENI into existence and gave Mattei the exclusive right to explore and exploit petroleum resources in the Po Valley. The battle was not only long and hard but also very bitter, and it probably was here that Mattei acquired his hatred of the large international oil companies, rather than at the time of his later alleged rebuff from the Iran Consortium.

Many of the things which Mattei said during the fight for the Po later haunted him, especially his wild and unfounded claims of untold wealth in both oil and gas, made in order to arouse Italian public opinion in his favor. Oil never has been found in the Po Valley in commercial quantities, and the gas fields are probably past their peak and, even with care and rationing, may last only another decade.

Without the support of Finance Minister Vanoni and of De Gasperi himself, Mattei might very well have lost the battle; and if the United States government had put pressure on Italy to keep the Po open, it is doubtful if Mattei would have had his way. (It must be said to the credit of the United States that hands were kept off this explosive Italian situation over the Po oil rights.) Vanoni was a great help to Mattei in other ways also, and his support gave Mattei a measure of respectability, experience, and reputation of public spiritedness that might otherwise have been difficult to obtain. One of the main streets in ENI's great complex at Metanopoli is named in honor of Vanoni, who cooled somewhat in his ardor for Mattei after the Po battle was won, and died before it became clear what Mattei had in mind for ENI. It would be interesting to hear what this shy, intelligent, melancholic, and least demagogic man in Italian public life would say of ENI today.

The most influential argument in the battle of the Po was that of keeping foreigners out of Italian resources, but it should be noted that Italian private enterprise was excluded also. With some Italians, this result was more important than the exclusion of foreigners. On theoretical grounds, it was argued during (and has been argued since) the Po controversy that the restriction of exploration and exploitation to a public company was based on three premises. First, it is alleged that only a public company would guarantee the development of a national resource without restrictive practices. This is the traditional Italian argument for the nationalization of industry. Though there is little evidence to support it, this view is based on the familiar socialist assumption that a public monopoly will, necessarily, be less inclined to restrictive practices than competing private companies. Second, the state receives the profits of the enterprise and can devote them to national ends. (In the case of ENI, however, the Ente kept the profits from the methane and devoted them to Mattei's ends.) Third, a public monopoly eliminates the possibility of a private monopoly or of undue concentration

Private monopoly and concentration can be dealt with in ways other than nationalizing or granting a public monopoly, though none of them ever has been tried in Italy. A public monopoly, especially on the present Italian scene, simply assures the presence of the very problems that are sought to be eliminated or avoided. Certainly, a private monopolist would be hard pressed to duplicate Mattei's monopolistic behavior.

Much of the discussion behind the new Italian Oil Law of 1957 [8] followed the same lines as the Po dispute, but, on the surface, the new law is considerably more lenient. Although it confirms the ENI monopoly in the Po Valley, it permits exploration and exploitation by private oil companies, both Italian and foreign, in other parts of Italy—even though under terms which, when analyzed, prove to be singularly unattractive.[9] The effect of the new law has been that private oil companies, including Italian, have abandoned exploration on the mainland leaving a clear field to ENI. Sicily, under the Italian scheme of regional autonomy, has its own oil law, and there the Gulf Oil Corporation operates the biggest and best oil field in Italy, but it has been under constant attack from Mattei and from the Communists.[10]

The Pipelines

Regardless of which side of the Po battle one might have had sympathy for, there is at least one bit of hindsight that would seem to confirm, on highly pragmatic grounds, the wisdom of giving the victory to Mattei. For a period of several years before the 1953 statute gave legal sanction to Mattei's monopoly, Mattei enjoyed a virtual monopoly in fact. Before the Po oil strikes, no one was very much interested in the Po Valley, and there were few concessions outstanding. After the strikes, and while the battle was raging, no new concessions were granted. Mattei had almost undisputed possession of most of the potential area and did not waste time before sinking as many wells in as many places as was feasible. Thus the fields were being developed while the decision was being made.

Gambling on his ultimate success, Mattei often sank wells without any legal right to do so and behaved in the same high-handed fashion that he so strenuously condemned in the foreign companies. But Mattei faced a serious problem. I believe that he was convinced rather early in the game that there was little oil in the Po Valley, and that what he had on his hands were several excellent methane fields. His problem was how to get the methane to market. Methane can be bottled, but to market it only in bottles is like dipping up the Mississippi with a teaspoon. The markets for the methane were in the industrial cities of the north —Milan, Turin, and the others—not far away from the fields by American standards but far enough away to make major pipeline construction necessary.

Italian law had no provision for the condemnation of rights-of-way for pipelines; [11] consequently any company seeking to provide pipeline transportation for the production of its gas fields was faced with the appalling task of negotiating contracts with thousands of small landowners and dozens of local governments and municipalities. Attempts to build pipelines in this fashion probably would still be in the negotiation stage. Mattei built the pipelines first and negotiated afterward. His personality, his nationality, and his immense public reputation made it possible for him to do what nobody else, and certainly no foreign oil company, could even have attempted. One can only imagine what the Communists, who were very strong in the Po Valley at the end of the war, would have done had Standard Oil of New Jersey tried to build the pipeline first and negotiate afterward. No one could accuse Mattei of being a "foreigner" or a "dirty imperialist, colonialist, capitalist exploiter of the masses."

Legends abound in northern Italy on how Mattei built the pipelines. The theme is the same in all of them: Mattei simply ignored private and public rights and the law. He boasts of having broken eight thousand ordinances and laws, and this must be a very conservative figure. Much of the work was done at night on the theory that by morning the work would be so far along there would not be very much that anybody could do about it. Once the ditch was dug, the pipe laid and the ditch refilled, the wound was not usually a very impressive one. When serious opposition arose, Mattei often appeared on the scene himself, full of apologies for his line crews who had "acted in error and without instructions," but "wouldn't it be a shame to have to dig it all up now?" The mayor of Cremona is reputed to have awakened one morning to find his town bisected by AGIP's nocturnal ditch digging and traffic completely paralyzed; he was so glad to get traffic restored that he agreed to rights-of-way on the spot. Mattei not only found the gas, but he also built the pipeline, and it is doubtful if anybody else, at that time, could have done the same.

Methane is still the foundation of ENI's vast industrial empire. It provides large profits; it is the basic raw material for the great chemical complex at Ravenna, where ENI makes the synthetic rubber which is traded to the Soviets for crude oil; and it supplies the energy for Italy's modern industrial "miracle." Without methane, there would be no ENI. Mattei's remarkable achievement with methane is enough, by itself, to remember him by, but it may not be enough to support the great inverted pyramid he erected upon it. The present and the future of ENI still depend on natural gas, because, unfortunately, ENI is still trying to be a major international oil company without any oil. We shall return to methane in Chapters 3 and 4 and try to find out why the profits are so large, where they come from, and how they are used.

OIL AND OIL-LESSNESS

Important though it was to Italy's postwar industrial revival and to the future of Mattei's operations, the Po Valley natural gas was no long-run solution to Italy's energy problems, a fact which Mattei probably understood better than anyone else. During the period related above, Mattei was still only managing director of AGIP, one of several state-owned companies engaged in various phases of the petroleum industry. With his usual passion for exclusive possession of any activity which he happened to be carrying on, but also for the purpose of continuing the search for solutions to Italy's energy shortage and to supply the burgeoning gasoline demands of AGIP's large distribution network, Mattei sought to bring all the state's petroleum activities under one head.

With the help of Vanoni, he drafted the Law of February 10, 1953, which brought ENI, a holding company, into existence,[12] transferred to it as subsidiaries the old state companies, AGIP, ANIC, ROMSA, and SNAM,[13] assigned to it the assets of the old companies, added a 24 million dollar cash contribution by the government,[14] and gave himself monopoly in the Po Valley.[15] Enrico Mattei was appointed president of the company [16] thus created.

No Oil in Italy

The creation of ENI gave Mattei a much better organizational tool, exclusive control of all government petroleum activities, and a monopoly of exploration and exploitation in the Po Valley, but did not solve the problem of how to provide petroleum products for his rapidly growing distribution system. Into the new ENI group ANIC brought two small out-of-date refineries, at Leghorn and Bari, and Mattei worked out a partnership arrangement with Standard Oil of New Jersey whereby Jersey was to enlarge and modernize the refineries in exchange for a 50 per cent interest therein. However, these two improved refineries, along with several other small ones under ENI's control, could provide only a small proportion of Mattei's own needs. The earlier claims of vast "Texas-sized" deposits of oil in the Po Valley became somewhat embarrassing, as no oil had been found and Mattei was now curtly denying that there was any oil there and at the same time refusing to others the right to look for it. This was neither the first nor the last example of paradoxical conduct, but I suspect that Mattei was convinced all along that the Po had no oil and that he did not expect much more in Italy as a whole. At any rate, he now turned to Iran.

Iran

Mattei let it be believed that he approached the Iran Consortium with a request for a small participation and was insultingly rebuffed. In 1952 Mossadegh nationalized the Iranian oil industry, until then owned and controlled by the Anglo-Iranian Oil Company, a British-owned concern that had been in Iran under one

name or another for more than fifty years; but the Iranians found
themselves unable to operate the industry or market its products.
In 1954 the Iranian government negotiated an agreement with a
group of foreign oil companies,[17] known as the Iran Consortium,
whereby they were to take over the operation of the wells and
refineries. It was in this arrangement that Mattei desired participation. He never furnished details of his request or of the refusal,
but it is commonly believed that the approach was made through
the offices of the then American ambassador, J. D. Zellerbach.
All Mattei ever said was that he was turned down in a way
"shameful and humiliating to Italy."

No one has been able to establish any of the facts in connection
with this alleged request and rebuff. A commentator in Italy said
recently that he could "deny categorically that Mattei ever made
such a request. He was not refused; he only feared that he would
be." [18] If Mattei did not actually make the request for participation, why did he say that he did? One possible reason is that
Mattei needed to explain why he was spending large sums of
Italian capital outside of Italy, and running great risks in a search
for oil, without making an effort to work out some arrangement
with the big international companies for an adequate supply.
Mattei probably would not have been content with what he considered to be the less dignified position of dealer in oil rather
than that of producer. If this first insult never took place, however, others did occur. The big oil producers, not surprisingly,
look down upon small oil producers and dealers and see few
reasons why they should be taken into the inner councils or even
considered when important oil policies are being settled. In the
international oil business, one's status is measured by one's production. Undiplomatic remarks and actions, especially after Mattei's constant attacks on private business and "foreign giants,"
should not have been unexpected and were simply the result of
Mattei's having been Italy's oil boss without any oil of his own.

If Mattei could not compete with the big international companies in terms of oil, he could compete in Italian politics and
in diplomacy. His monopoly in the Po Valley was achieved, and
Mattei was pleased with his steadily increasing share of the Italian

gasoline market and with the Oil Law of 1957, although these did
not compare in satisfaction with victory that might be won on
the international level. This is probably the chief reason that that
same year Mattei entered the Iranian scene with such force and
energy.

What he sought were concessions in Iran in areas not already
granted to the Consortium. If oil was his objective, he did not
achieve very much, but if shocking the "seven sisters" was his
purpose, he succeeded brilliantly. The members of the Consortium fought Mattei's entry into Iran with all the tools at their
command, but Mattei played his cards well and again obtained
what he wanted. In 1957 he got concessions in Iran, and the terms
of the contract with the Iranian government gave the major oil
companies some jolts they would not soon forget.

Unfortunately, Mattei's big diplomatic achievements in Iran
and elsewhere were not matched by his findings of "big oil." It
would be a mistake to assume that Mattei sought oil only for the
purpose of teaching the big oil companies a lesson. As will be discussed in greater detail, ENI always has needed oil and needed
it badly; ENI's whole future may depend on finding it and finding
it soon. There is strong evidence to suggest that Mattei's preoccupation with vengeance, as well as his disadvantageous concession agreements and attempts to avoid large bonus payments that
might be embarrassing at home, led him to spread his search efforts
too thin and to devote too much time and money to new, fringe,
or unpromising areas. In contrast, the Japanese,[19] recently entering the international petroleum arena for the first time since the
end of World War II, paid a very high price for offshore rights
in the Neutral Zone, the most promising petroleum area in the
world, and hit "big oil" almost immediately. ENI is still searching.
Mattei found oil in Egypt, where the oil[20] and the contract
terms[21] are amazingly bad; in Libya, where in 1961 he apparently
found a fairly good deposit;[22] in Iran, but in small quantities; in
Sicily at Gela, where the quantity is satisfactory but the quality
is little better than that of bitumen; and elsewhere—but the combined total still is insignificant. ENI's production in 1963 may have
reached four million tons. Italy's needs alone, for 1962, have been

estimated at twenty-two million tons, and world production in
1960 was more than one billion tons. Such was the embarrassment
and the predicament of the big oil tycoon without "big oil."

In Mattei's eyes, production was only part of the story. He
maintained his reputation and position at home and had considerable success in building a reputation in Africa, South America, and
in the Middle East, although disillusionment was setting in for
parts of the latter area.[23] Mattei's public relations skill was one of
his most valuable assets, both at home and abroad. His public
image, especially in Italy and Africa, was that of the little St.
George fighting the international oil dragon. Though ENI now
has assets of almost two billion dollars [24] and annual sales of 650
million dollars, the image persists.

Mattei talked as though he considered his Iran concession in
1957 as his major triumph, and in some ways it was. The "seven
sisters" reacted as though Iran had nationalized the oil industry
again. The greatest shock appeared to be the introduction of what
amounts to a 75-25 formula for profit sharing. The 50-50 pattern
had become the standard of the industry after its introduction in
Venezuela in the 1940's and in the Middle East by Aramco in
1950. When the 75-25 formula burst on the Middle East oil scene
in 1957, there were loud cries of impending chaos. Actually, the
two formulas do not add up very differently. Mattei's 75-25 pattern
does not include bonus payments that almost invariably accompany other agreements and does not require ENI to support civic
improvements, highways, housing, education, and other activities
often a part of the concessionaire's responsibilities. Of course, the
oil companies were aware of this but were afraid that they might
be put under pressure to adopt the 75-25 pattern in addition to all
the other undertakings. Mattei worked very hard to get his
Iranian concessions. He induced a state visit by the President of
Italy to help the cause along and is alleged to have offered a
princess from the House of Savoy as a wife for the Shah, but
what he really did was to offer the Iranians a contract that gave
them the impression that they were participating in the production of oil. As much as at anything, the international oil companies were astounded that Mattei had learned in a very short

time how to beat them at a game they thought they had developed to perfection.

Mattei did not stop with Iran. His next visit was to Egypt,[25] where an absolutist government had nationalized industry. Playing his familiar anticapitalist role, Mattei obtained another unusual sort of contract with few, if any, advantages for Italy. He built a refinery in Morocco, to be jointly owned by ENI and the Moroccan government, and obtained the passage there of a law requiring that only petroleum locally refined in his SAMIR refinery be sold or distributed in Morocco. Is it only coincidence that Jersey Standard owned the largest number of distributive outlets in Morocco? Mattei's agents, if not Mattei himself, seemed to be on hand as each new African nation raised its flag for the first time.

Mattei did not confine his efforts to the underdeveloped portions of the world, or to the search for oil. AGIP invaded Britain in 1962, and, though Mattei denied it, there was little doubt that he intended introducing there the unfamiliar practice (to Britain) of price competition in petrol. Pipelines are being built through the Alps to Switzerland and Germany, as are refineries in both places.

NUCLEAR ENERGY AND RUSSIAN OIL

There was much talk a few years ago, especially in Italy, about how nuclear energy was going to replace all other forms and how there was an oil crisis in the world because too much was being produced and because nuclear power was soon to replace it. Mattei's public relations program contributed no little bit to the story; it made a good defense against charges that he was not producing much oil. The best evidence seems to indicate that it will be a great many years before nuclear energy can begin to replace or even compete with petroleum, and there is real danger that known supplies of petroleum may be exhausted before a replacement can be utilized. On one hand, ENI is building and will operate the first nuclear power station in Italy; on the other hand, ENI still does not have enough oil and, until recently, was trying desperately, short of going to the international petroleum companies, to obtain it. Perhaps Mattei's most controversial act after entering the petroleum scene was his negotiation of a contract to buy Russian crude. The Italian government had actually purchased small amounts of Russian oil for several years and was negotiating a renewal of this agreement when Mattei, without consulting his government, negotiated his own contract for twelve million tons of Russian oil over a period of four years, to be paid for with steel pipe and synthetic rubber to be supplied by Mattei.

Mattei has been accused of sabotaging NATO and the West, of buying political petroleum, of supplying strategic materials to the Soviets and of giving aid and comfort to the enemy; but actually he had very little choice. His grand commitments, his lack of supplies and his battle with the major oil companies left him with a serious problem. Opposition to the contract was strong, even in Italy, but Mattei defended himself by arguing that the Russian oil was very cheap (and lowered the price of his gasoline about one cent a gallon to prove it) [26] and that the arrangement was only temporary while he brought his own sources into production. Again Mattei took a serious risk.

Mattei tried by other means to increase his supplies of petroleum. The best oil field in Italy is Gulf's field at Ragusa, which alone produces almost as much crude as all of ENI's operations. Although Mattei denied that he wanted the Ragusa concession, it was obvious that its very presence in private and foreign hands rankled him considerably. There is good evidence that he encouraged the unsuccessful efforts of Sicily's Communist Deputies to have the Ragusa concession revoked. During the height of this attempt, during the fall of 1961, Mattei's newspaper, *Il Giorno*, led the fight against Gulf, with the help of the far-left press.

The Ragusa field was particularly irritating to Mattei because his own Sicilian field at Gela had been so disappointing. The Gela crude is difficult to handle and expensive to refine, but ENI is building at Gela a petrochemical plant, a thermoelectric plant, and a refinery. It is interesting to note, however, that the size and conformation of the piers also under construction there suggest that Mattei hoped, as soon as possible, to be refining his own Middle Eastern oil at Gela and to get out from under the unfor-

tunate Gela crude. The British Petroleum Company discovered
the Gela field but abandoned it because of the poor quality of
the oil. Mattei made much of the fact that ENI was a public
company and could not callously abandon Gela to its fate. A
public relations victory is, in this fashion, combined with a refinery and other facilities suited to the processing of imported
crude.

Had Mattei confined himself to petroleum, some of the most
interesting activities of ENI would not have developed. Though
the statute creating ENI describes its scope as "the field of hydrocarbons and natural vapors," [27] Mattei, with the skill of a Phila-
delphia lawyer, interpreted the language to cover a vast assort-
ment of activities, many of which are related only vaguely, if at
all, to hydrocarbons. Through one affiliated company or another,
ENI has been engaged in industries as various as motels, highways,
chemicals, soap, fertilizers, synthetic rubber, machinery, instruments, textiles, electrical generation and distribution, contract research, contract engineering and construction, publishing, nuclear
power and research, steel pipe, cement, carbon black, investment
banking, and even education, to mention only a few.[28] ENI recently acquired Lanerossi, a large wool textile firm in the Veneto,
for the purpose, according to Mattei, of providing an outlet for
the synthetic fibers to be produced at the Ferrandina gas fields in
Southern Italy. Mattei's enemies say his purpose was to get hold of
17,000 employees in the home district of a Christian Democratic
politician he did not already control.

Mattei and ENI are both paradoxes. An oil company without
oil manufactures soap and fertilizer, operates a woolen knitting
mill, and builds a nuclear power plant. A petroleum boss without
petroleum became a major influence in the international petroleum
industry, began the construction of a pipeline through the Alps
for petroleum he did not have, and provided almost one-third of
the gasoline required by Italian motorists. A government-owned
corporation operates a newspaper in order to influence public
opinion against interference by the government. An antimonopolist sought to drive out competition wherever he found it.
A public corporation is subject to audit by no one. A civil servant

dominated the government by which he was employed. An anti-capitalist conducted his affairs in close imitation of the capitalist robber barons of a half century ago. From origins in a defunct fascist oil company, ENI has grown into a vast billion-dollar industrial complex. From a minor public official who was charged with the responsibility, in 1946, of liquidating the assets of a small public corporation, Mattei grew into the most powerful man in Italy. This brief review of ENI and of Mattei will serve as a background for appraising their performance and examining the phenomenon in power which they represent.

CHAPTER 3

Background
of Power

From an outline of ENI's history, we now move to a detailed investigation of ENI's economic power and performance. This step is necessary both for the purpose of becoming acquainted with an arena in which much of ENI's and Mattei's power was manifested and also in order to take our first crude measurements of the scope and of some of the sources of that power. We shall see how ENI's financial statements were often more a matter of public relations than a matter of information and how Mattei employed his many forms of power to enhance ENI's economic posture. In the course of this investigation, we shall discover the secrets of ENI's fantastic growth and expansion, the sources of ENI's capital, and the circumstances in which actual performance was considerably at variance with apparent performance. All of these features are really just manifestations of the power wielded by Enrico Mattei. In Chapter 4 we shall take a closer look at the apparatus through and by which the power was exercised.

The appraisal of the economic performance of ENI must rely, however, even more heavily than is usual in the case of public companies, on factors outside the financial statements. Most of these outside factors are related to the legal, political, and social environment in which ENI operates, but all of them played a role in the development of the power exercised by Mattei and by his company.

It may be said in a general way that profit cannot and should not be the major criterion of a public company's performance.

Indeed, in many cases, profits, especially substantial profits, might be good evidence of the failure of a mission rather than of its success. We cannot, therefore, conclude that the financial statements may be ignored when appraising the performance of a public company. A profit or a loss may be subject to somewhat different interpretations in the financial statement of a public company than in comparable statements of private companies, but the statements may contain, nonetheless, relevant and useful information. Furthermore, the balance sheets may be of considerable help in analyzing the growth characteristics of the enterprise, the disposition of its capital, the efficiency with which assets are utilized, and in taking rough measurements of its economic power. The published balance sheets of ENI can be used as a basis for certain useful deductions, but the profit and loss statements are almost totally without value, beginning, as many of them do, with "gross profit" and ending a half dozen items later with a "net profit." The profit and loss statements of the subsidiary and affiliated companies take the same form and contain the same dearth of information. (See Exhibit A) In addition, it must be said that the lack of true audit by government or any independent agency destroys most of the confidence that might otherwise be placed in the financial statements.

The lack of reliable financial statements and of substantial reports to the government affects this appraisal at every turn. It is extremely difficult to find a bit of solid ground on which to stand and from which to begin an examination of ENI's activities and organization. It is very easy on one hand to ascertain from the ENI reports how many meters of wells have been sunk in the last year or decade and which countries now enjoy AGIP service stations or motels, but on the other hand it is impossible to find out ENI's estimates of the size of the Po Valley methane reserves, the exact terms of its contract with the Egyptian government, its profits on any operation or how they are determined, or what is really intended for the expensive installations now being built at Gela. Although Mattei and other ENI officials insisted that Mattei consulted regularly with the government before making im-

EXHIBIT A

AGIP MINERARIA PROFIT AND LOSS STATEMENT

December 31, 1959 (figures rounded)

	Lire (000,000)
Costs and Losses	
General Costs of Administration	2,870
Financing Costs	4,477
Diverse and Extraordinary Costs	2,140
Tax and Other Tributary Costs	1,327
Amortization and Depreciation	6,112
	16,928
Profits and Receipts	
Gross Profit	17,843
Financing Receipts	235
Miscellaneous Receipts	758
	18,836
	16,928
NET PROFIT	1,908

portant moves, it cannot be discovered with whom he consulted, in what form, what he said, or what kind of response he received. All that is known is that the committee of ministers which was originally expected to supervise ENI's operations kept no minutes of its meetings and apparently did nothing except transmit the reports it received from Mattei. The Ministry of State Participations, created to replace this committee of ministers, occasionally issues statements on ENI and its performance, but these statements are almost invariably based on unaudited reports submitted by the Ente itself. Much of what is thought to be known about ENI is based on rumors, unfounded charges by Mattei's enemies, and on publications and press releases issued by ENI's own public relations office. As far as is possible we shall seek to distinguish between facts and reasonably well-supported conclusions on one hand and conjecture on the other. It will not be easy.

ECONOMIC POWER

No appraisal of the performance of ENI would be complete
without at least an attempt to penetrate or to look around the
edges of the veil of unaudited annual reports and financial statements. These documents cannot be used in the same way that
they would be used if issued by an American private corporation
and, by themselves, are not a satisfactory guide to ENI's economic
performance, but we are not necessarily led to the conclusion
that the reports should be ignored or that they are totally without value. Actually, when augmented with personal observations
and collateral information, the annual reports do provide some
useful data and can be employed as a basis for certain reasonably
tenable conclusions. If, for example, one is willing to scan one
source for the price of Po Valley methane, another source for
ENI's production of that commodity, and apply to these bits of
data a cost figure computed from information available from
other producers elsewhere, one can arrive at a workable estimate
of the profits that ENI has been enjoying from its Po Valley gas.

The marvels of the ENI reports have been observed for many
years and have become part of the folklore surrounding the company. It has been said [1] that one observer, after many fruitless
attempts to decipher the ENI reports, sent sets of them to a firm
of chartered accountants in London and to a certified public accounting firm in New York, but even these august examiners of
company accounts admitted defeat. Mattei's response to these
stories, and there are several versions, was that "a modest book-
keeper just out of school" [2] could have provided the answers, and
"one need only consult page 25, 42, or 96" of a particular report
in order to obtain the necessary information. Many people have
rushed eagerly to the designated pages, thinking that perhaps
they had been guilty of an oversight, only to find the usual "consolidated balance sheet" or income statement occupying less than
one-fourth of a page.

Because this study is one of power, not of economic performance, consideration will be given to economic phenomena only

to the extent necessary to enlarge or improve the background against which the power phenomena will later be appraised. Among the areas which meet the tests both of relevance to the basic purpose of this study and of accessibility are the following, which will be given brief attention below: 1) growth, expansion, and diversification; 2) pricing policies; 3) sources of capital; 4) ENI as an antimonopolistic force; and 5) ENI's performance in the Mezzogiorno. Although unaudited statements are always suspect, it should be recognized here that most of the attacks on the ENI reports have charged not outright falsification but omission. Much of the relevant information simply is not mentioned at all. For the purposes of this brief discussion of ENI's economic performance, it will be assumed that the data appearing in the financial statements are reasonably accurate, so far as they go; the question of the reliability of the statements is discussed elsewhere.

Growth, Expansion, and Diversification

It is not difficult to trace, in a number of different ways, the fantastic growth of ENI since its formation in 1953.[3] The growth revealed on the record probably understates the actual situation considerably. In order to conceal the size of the Po Valley natural gas profits and the uses to which they have been put, the ENI financial statements have been made consistent with a low profit level in natural gas, and the expansion of the Group's assets has been attributed largely to borrowed funds. Even the understatement is impressive, however. The assets of ENI alone increased from 30 billion lire [4] in 1953 to 293 billion in 1962,[5] and the consolidated assets of the Group from approximately 60 billion lire in 1953 to 955 billion in 1962. Sales by the Group have not kept pace, rising from 215.5 billion lire in 1955, the end of the first full year of operation, to 406 billion in 1962. Employment within the Group has risen from 17,601 in 1956, the first year for which reliable figures are available, to 47,804 at the end of 1961. In late summer, 1962, Mattei claimed 50,000 employees for the ENI Group.

When Enrico Mattei became managing director of AGIP in

TABLE 1

Production of Hydrocarbons in Italy

Year	Liquid (Tons)		Methane (ooo Cubic Meters)	
	E.N.I.	*Other*	*E.N.I.*	*Other*
1946	2,691	8,528	12,597	51,451
1947	2,911	7,933	19,641	73,861
1948	2,551	7,131	28,118	88,994
1949	3,630	6,375	106,581	142,851
1950	5,079	4,904	305,699	203,929
1951	17,075	4,367	723,583	242,689
1952	85,617	4,575	1,171,114	256,188
1953	132,057	3,801	2,006,822	272,856
1954	123,820	5,997	2,700,400	266,869
1955	114,851	145,509	3,343,273	283,970
1956	134,828	496,319	4,158,736	306,539
1957	216,706	1,110,552	4,684,683	302,391
1958	345,406	1,253,879	4,821,712	353,958
1959	364,065	1,391,274	5,759,331	358,218
1960	673,362	1,383,711	6,167,888	279,336
1961	556,698	1,472,080	6,667,981	194,729

1946, the company was producing natural gas at the rate of 12.6 million cubic meters per annum. By the time ENI was brought into existence in 1953, production was up to two billion cubic meters; production reached 6.2 billion in 1960. In 1961, the production increased to 6.7 billion cubic meters, but the spectacular rate of growth of earlier years had come to an end. Table 1 shows the production each year from 1946 through 1961. New fields in Italy may eventually raise the total to 8.5 or nine billion. The record of ENI's production of liquid petroleum in Italian fields is neither spectacular nor very significant, and is unlikely ever to attract much attention. Even if the Gela field moves into full production (and there are real doubts because of the low quality of the crude that it is ever seriously expected to do so), ENI's total in Italy probably will not much exceed three million tons a year.[6] Only in the event that ENI succeeds in taking over the Gulf field at Ragusa would its Italian production be worthy of note, and not even then by Middle Eastern standards. At the most optimistic production levels, all the Italian oil fields combined could not supply more than one-fifth of Italy's own needs. ENI's production outside Italy is not yet significant, and production from all of ENI's sources at home and abroad may have reached, at the most, four million tons in 1963.

Since 1948, ENI has increased its share of the Italian gasoline market from 15 per cent to almost 30 per cent in spite of a sevenfold growth in the consumption of gasoline. Most of the increase in market share can be attributed to two factors: modern marketing techniques and skillful encouragement of nationalistic tendencies. ENI brought modern service stations to Italy; Mattei's advertising and public relations efforts emphasized the antiforeign and pro-Italian theme. ENI's sales abroad cannot be ascertained with any degree of accuracy. The annual reports avoid discussion of sales figures and rarely disclose more than percentages of overall increase or decrease. ENI has petroleum marketing outlets in Europe, Africa, the Middle East, and in South America, but no sales figures, by country or product, are available.

Were our story to end here, the only support for our use of the appellation "spectacular" in regard to ENI's growth would have to be sought in the asset growth, not matched by sales, in the rapid development of the Po Valley gas fields, and in the increased share of the Italian gasoline market. Perhaps the most remarkable aspect of ENI's development, however, is its extensive vertical integration. Loaded as the old fascist AGIP was with overaged and underskilled functionaries, this predecessor of ENI had no measurable success in its primary field of petroleum exploration, production, processing, and sales—and even less in collateral or supporting areas in which it was engaged. AGIP's technical staff, except for a few highly talented young men on whom Mattei relied heavily during his first years with the company, was not brilliant and had no bent toward organization. Planning, design, engineering, and refining were, with a few exceptions, carried on with magnificent inefficiency and incompetence. Relations with suppliers and customers were uniformly poor.

The lesson of the AGIP experience undoubtedly caused Mattei to take a totally different tack once control was his. He immediately began to promote the young, aggressive, and skillful men into the key positions in the company, to emphasize training, and as the personnel and organization became available to see to it that more and more collateral activities were performed within the company itself. He insisted that AGIP, and later ENI, acquire well-trained geophysicists; petroleum, refinery, and reservoir engineers; draftsmen and chemists; and other technicians whose services are so important to a petroleum company. His design and project engineering staff became so good that its services are in demand all over Italy and over a large portion of the world. From these activities, the ENI Group soon moved into building its own refineries, plants, and installations and developed, in SAIPEM, one of the largest industrial contracting and engineering firms in the world. When ENI today wishes to build a petrochemical plant, one subsidiary perfects the process which another subsidiary adapts for actual production; still another designs the installation and estimates its costs; another subsidiary builds the plant; yet another takes over its operation. Under the circumstances, the performance of most of these activities within the organization makes very good sense indeed. In this fashion, Mattei insulated ENI from many of the service and supply portions of the economy and obtained for himself and his company much greater independence and flexibility than otherwise would have been the case.

ENI did not stop there. Instead of buying petroleum machinery, instruments, and equipment, ENI purchased the semi-defunct Nuovo Pignone factory in Florence and began to supply its own needs for these products and also to sell to other users. Pipe, pumps and valves, drills and rigging, prefabricated service stations, and a huge variety of other equipment is now being manufactured by the ENI Group. From integration backward, Mattei turned to integration forward and began to build or buy petrochemical, thermoelectric, and other types of installations that use petroleum as a raw material or a fuel. ENI now produces urea, nitrogenous and complex fertilizers, cis-polybutadiene

rubber, latex, carbon black, polyvinyl chloride, ammonia, poly-
ethelene, several polymers, and electricity. Activities once carried
on but now disposed of include soap and detergents, fats and
margarine, and sensitized paper. Shortly after these activities
were disposed of, in order to bring "their operations into fundamental fields of activity—refining, petrochemicals, and fertilizers,"
ENI acquired a woolen knitting mill, purportedly as an outlet
for its synthetic fibers. Two ENI companies are searching for and
exploiting sources of potassium salts, required in the manufacture
of fertilizers, and another carries on the research necessary before the salts can be extracted from the mineral.[7]

The drive into fields more and more remotely related to petroleum has continued without letup. One ENI subsidiary is
building, and another ENI company will operate, Italy's first
nuclear power station; still another ENI company is designing a
second nuclear power plant. Members of the ENI Group are
designing, locating, supplying materials for, and building and
operating motels all over Italy. Others are designing, providing
materials for, building, and even providing land for highways
and freeways. ENI subsidiaries are manufacturing alternating
compressors, engine-compressors, industrial refrigeration units
(for which the Soviet Union appears to be the largest customer)
centrifugal compressors, gas turbines, pneumatic, electric, me-
chanical and electronic meters, cement, light fabricated goods of
aluminum, steel and other metals, and other products too numerous to mention. In addition, ENI owns a newspaper, *Il
Giorno*.[8] Mattei also carried on his own foreign aid program.
ENI extended a 120 million dollar credit to India for the development of its petroleum industry, and made similar arrangements in Argentina and Brazil. A large proportion of the credits,
however, was to be spent on Italian petroleum machinery and
equipment, the chief supplier of which is ENI's own Nuovo
Pignone.

As has been pointed out repeatedly, many of ENI's collateral
activities are uneconomic, as are some of the operations within
the area of its primary responsibility. Spectacular though the
drive into nonbasic hydrocarbon industries has been, the economic

results, with some exceptions, are not satisfactory. Gela has been
labeled "uneconomic" by experts inside and outside the company
and even by Mattei, when he was not trying to prove some contrary point. The evidence available on the massive petrochemical
complex at Ravenna has led both insiders and outsiders to question its economic justification. However, I am not at all sure that
valid conclusions could be based on any sort of financial statements, no matter how accurate, reliable, or detailed. The city of
Ravenna, for example, before Mattei came, was as dead as any
city can become. It existed only on the tourists who came to
enjoy its lovely but decaying churches, buildings, and streets; it
offered nothing for its young people in the way of a future and
many of them departed. Now, all is changed. It would be difficult
to find a more lively, aggressive, forward-looking city anywhere
in Italy: the harbor, which had been silted up for years, is
operating again; the idle men who once filled the sidewalks and
piazzas are gone; the atmosphere is no longer one of decay but
rather of vitality and energy. ENI can take credit for the change.
One can bear a great deal of "uneconomic" behavior and a considerable amount of high-handed conduct if what happened in
Ravenna is the result. Whether the resurrection of Italy's Ravennas
should be left to the whim of uncontrolled modern *condottieri*
is a genuine issue in Italy, but it is not by any means certain how
much the presence of that issue should be allowed to detract
from Mattei's accomplishments. The least that can be said is that
on many economic grounds, not all of them measured in lire and
tons, the performance of ENI has been truly spectacular.

Pricing Policies

Natural gas. In three areas ENI's pricing practices and policies
are worth examining: Po Valley natural gas, fuel oil, and gasoline.
ENI bases the price of one cubic meter of its natural gas on the
price of the quantity of fuel oil needed to produce the same
amount of heat; included in the price of the fuel oil is a very
high Italian tax on that product. The exact details of how this
price equivalence is worked out are not known and are never
mentioned in ENI publications. We do know that the price of

Po Valley natural gas for industrial use has for some time been
in the neighborhood of twelve lire per cubic meter. Why is this
method of pricing used? There are two possible answers. The answer invariably used by ENI in defending itself against its critics
is that to have priced the Po gas near its cost would have further
increased the economic advantages which the North of Italy already enjoys over the South. Although this reason originally may
have been the explanation for the pricing system, especially during the time that Senator Vanoni was a supporter of Mattei and
ENI, several factors now suggest that the real reason was to increase ENI's profits.

The first factor that makes us suspicious that the protection of
the south is not the only reason for tying the price of Po methane
to the price of fuel oil is the relatively high price of the fuel
oil itself. Mattei frequently condemned the large international oil
companies for extracting exorbitant profits from their sales of fuel
oil and blamed the price of his methane on them. However, ENI
sells almost five million tons of fuel oil in Italy each year and made
no move, even after the Russian oil deal, to bring down the price
of that product, which if anything is more easily available in
Southern Italy than in the North. As a matter of fact, there is
some evidence that Mattei encouraged an increase in the price of
fuel oil about the time he was lowering the price of gasoline in
order to gain support for his oil contract with the USSR. Furthermore, there is no record of Mattei's ever having recommended
a reduction in the heavy tax on fuel oil; actually, Mattei is said
to have sought an increase in the tax at one time in order to keep
the price of methane from following a downward trend in the
price of fuel oil. The obvious fact is that as long as the profits
from the Po gas loom so large in the ENI picture, it will be against
the company's best interests to do anything which might tend
to reduce the price of fuel oil and, thus, the price of methane.

Further support of the view that the profits are the primary
reason for the Po pricing methods was seen in Mattei's failure to
reduce the price of fuel oil even after he began to obtain the
Russian crude at prices which, according to Mattei, were much
lower than those offered by the big Western companies. Because

the Russian oil contract is a barter arrangement, it is difficult to attach a price to the Russian crude oil. With a little interpolation, one can arrive at a price in the range between $1.00 and $1.15 a barrel, about one-third less than the Middle Eastern price. ENI supplies from its own resources most of the bartered goods, however, so costs and prices cannot be accurately fixed and, consequently, lose most of their relevance.

A second factor lending credence to the profit motive, as opposed to the protection of the South, is the current availability of natural gas supplies in several areas of the Mezzogiorno. Little progress has been made in developing outlets for the gas, and price is conspicuously absent from discussions of the future of the natural gas fields in Southern Italy. Most of the gas being used or shortly scheduled to be used from these fields is going to members of the ENI Group, with regard to whom price is not a major factor. There is no evidence that the gas from the southern fields will be made available at anything other than the price formula already in use in the Po Valley. The very secrecy with which the Po prices are determined, the total absence of Po Valley sales and profits figures from the financial statements of the company, and the dense fog that is always thrown up when the Po profits are mentioned by outsiders, are, at the very least, evidence of acute sensitivity in that area—sensitivity that cannot be explained if protection of the South is the primary motive for the gas pricing formula.

The Po Valley gas is not exorbitantly priced, in spite of the fact that the prices are set somewhat arbitrarily, as well as mysteriously, and are probably two or three times the cost of producing and delivering to the consumer. The Po gas could have been priced much higher than it was. ENI had a complete monopoly in the producing area of the North and a virtual monopoly of the means of transporting the gas to the areas of use, and the advantages of natural gas over fuel oil, for most purposes, would have supported a higher price for the gaseous fuel. Up to the point where consumers would begin to shift to fuel oil or other sources of energy, the Po gas, whatever its price, saves Italy almost eighty billion lire a year in foreign exchange, at present near-maximum levels of production. However, unless wholly un-expected sources of natural gas are discovered in Northern Italy, the present supplies appear to be adequate for only another ten to twelve years.

Fuel oil. The steadily and rapidly increasing Italian energy re-quirements are now being met from fuel oil imports and not from natural gas. This probably will continue to be the pattern until some still far-distant date when nuclear sources become easily and economically available. In the meantime, the price of fuel oil in Italy may be of much greater long-run importance than the price of natural gas. In fuel oil, however, ENI does not have a monopoly of the supply (although it is an important trader in the Italian market), and has only limited influence on market be-havior. So long as the price of Po Valley or other Italian methane is tied to the price of fuel oil, so long as the supplies of natural gas are an important factor in the Italian energy situation, and so long as the ENI colossus depends as heavily as it now does on the natural gas profits, the influence of ENI on the price of fuel oil is likely to be exerted in an upward rather than in a downward direction.

Gasoline. In sharp contrast with its pricing policies in regard to methane and fuel oil, at least on the surface, are ENI's pricing policies for gasoline. If one accepts the image which ENI's public relations efforts seek to construct, it was ENI's price reductions in 1960 which, "by widening consumption . . . permitted the government to reduce gasoline taxes so that within a short span of time the price of gasoline fell from 142 to 96 lire per liter," [9] brought about sharply increased sales, not only of gasoline and related products, but also of motor vehicles.

"The substantial drops in prices were the result of AGIP's efforts to bring prices down which upset the former oligopolistic balance which the international companies were trying to maintain in Italy, in spite of lower crude oil prices and freight rates arising out of the changeover from a sellers' to a buyers' market. AGIP carried out this task successfully in Italy. An initial reduction in price from Lit. 128 to Lit. 125 per litre was approved by the interministerial Price Committee—CIP on 15th May 1959. On

19th March 1960 AGIP cut its price to Lit. 120 on its own initiative, followed a few days later by the other companies. On 22nd May 1960 the manufacturing tax was lowered and the official price was reduced by CIP to Lit. 100. In August 1960 AGIP once again, off its own bat, lowered the price by Lit. 2 but this time the other companies did not follow suit. Two prices, AGIP's Lit. 98 and the Lit. 100 of the other companies, continued to exist side by side until 1st February of this year when the manufacturing tax was again reduced and the official price became Lit. 96 per litre." [10]

Closer examination of the circumstances, however, reveals several reasons why the facts may not justify the conclusions and the image. The conclusion that competitive price reductions by AGIP were all that were necessary to bring down the total price of gasoline by substantial steps has some weaknesses. In the first place, the "initial reduction" referred to in the paragraph above was made by the government, not by AGIP, though the construction of the paragraph and sentence tends to leave the opposite impression; furthermore, the government had also made a substantial reduction in tax in the preceding year. AGIP made no reduction until March, 1960, ten months later, when it cut the price by five lire. Less than two months later, a rather short time for the "widening consumption" to have become known and for the government to have acted, the government reduced the price by twenty lire. AGIP cut two more lire in August, 1960, and the government four more in February, 1961. Between May, 1959, and February, 1961, then, AGIP had reduced the price of gasoline by seven lire, and the government had reduced the tax by twenty-seven lire.[11] Who took the initiative and whose cuts brought about the increased consumption are open to question. It is likely, however, that Mattei's direct personal pressure on the interministerial Price Committee was a major factor in the government's actions.

Other mitigating factors should be mentioned also. The tax on gasoline sold in Italy has been so high (now about $0.40 per gallon, 69.83 lire per liter, or over 70 per cent of the price) that the nontax portion of the total price has become relatively unimportant. Long before ENI entered the stage, the nontax gasoline price in Italy was low, lower in fact than almost anywhere else in the world, including the United States. The profit margins of the oil companies operating in Italy were not large to begin with, and the seven-lire price reduction by AGIP in 1960 probably has pushed some of them into the red so far as gasoline sales are concerned. My conclusion, based on refining and transportation costs of other companies, and other evidence, is that AGIP, except for intercompany billings within the ENI Group, lost money on gasoline too. The timing of the two-lire reduction in August, 1960, coupled with the kind of public relations announcements which accompanied and followed it, tend to support the view that the price cut was motivated, not by the competitive instincts proclaimed by ENI, but by the desire to create a favorable atmosphere for the Russian oil contract.

Sources of Capital

The most popular mystery in ENI's variegated panoply of mysteries is: "Where does the money come from?" The growth of ENI has been so rapid and so spectacular that one is not surprised when myths and mysteries arise to explain it. The wonder is that the mystery of the sources of capital has persisted over such a considerable period when information with which to dispel it has long been available; and the solution is neither clever nor unexpected. Apparently acting on the theory that it is more fun to have a mystery than to solve it, observers have largely ignored the evidence that was available. It cannot be said that one need only read ENI's annual reports to find the answers to our query, but it is accurate to say that therein lies the key. The ENI reports being what they are, it is not possible to match lira for lira the growth of the company with the sources of capital, but one can make good approximations.

In the Po Valley profits we search for our first clue, to the surprise of no one. Table 1 (page 30) shows the production of natural gas by ENI during the period 1946 to 1961. It should be noted that production reached the level of two billion cubic meters per annum in the year that ENI came into existence. The price of the natural gas, discussed above, can reasonably be placed at twelve lire per cubic meter. Many expert guesses have been made as to the cost of Mattei's methane, based on experience in the United States and elsewhere, and range from less than five lire per cubic meter to seven lire. I am inclined to accept a figure in the lower range, say five lire. During the exchange between Indro Montanelli and Mattei in *Corriere della Sera* in the summer of 1961, Montanelli based his estimates of the Po Valley profits on a cost figure of five lire per cubic meter or "maybe a little less." When Mattei replied to Montanelli's charges, he challenged, either specifically or categorically, almost every allegation that Montanelli had made but said not a word about the Po Valley profits.[12] The resulting profit figure of seven lire per cubic meter means that Mattei had had at his disposal, since 1953, annual profits in rather substantial amounts, ranging from a low of 14 billion lire ($22,500,000) in 1953 to 46 billion ($74,000,000) in 1961. It will be noted that the estimated profits from natural gas in 1961 were more than seven times the amount of net profit actually reported to the government in that year: 6.2 billion lire. Over the nine-year period from 1953 to 1961, the Po gas profits must have amounted to something like 300 billion lire ($480,000,000).

It cannot be said with accuracy where the 300 billion went. Certainly, some of it went into assets which do not appear on the financial statements or are substantially undervalued. Much of the remainder was undoubtedly paid for the coöperation of the press, favorable treatment in the Middle East and Africa, support by politicians, and for a wide variety of similar advantages. It is obvious that only the complete lack of auditing and control procedures made it possible to conceal or omit from the financial statements sums in the amount of 300 billion lire, and it should be recognized that this figure is a relatively conservative estimate; some estimates run higher than 400 billion lire.

The Po gas profits make little impression on ENI's financial statements. True, AGIP Mineraria, which produces the gas, and SNAM, which distributes the gas, both wholly owned by ENI, show larger profits than AGIP and ANIC, the other two major ENI companies, but the total reported by the two of them is

less than one-tenth of the estimated Po profits, and both AGIP
Mineraria and SNAM have extensive operations outside the Po
Valley. AGIP Mineraria's profit and loss statement for 1959
(see Exhibit A, page 27) suggests how the disappearing act is
accomplished: the relevant portion of the statement begins with
a "gross profit" and reveals nothing with regard to sales or costs
of production.

The portion of ENI's asset growth that appears in its balance
sheets is easily explained by the data in Table 2. This table covers
the entire life of ENI and is based on the annual statements of that
company as verified by the statements of the more important
affiliated companies in the ENI Group. ENI's initial capital was
a government subsidy of thirty billion lire, consisting one-half of
cash and one-half of the conservatively valued assets of AGIP
and several other pre-existing companies merged into the ENI
Group in 1953. It is clear from this table that long-term borrowing, supplemented occasionally by bank loans, provided most of
the capital employed by the company, at least so far as the balance
sheet is concerned. It is clear also that most of the funds went
to the subsidiaries.

ENI has used two methods of distributing funds to the subsidiaries. The more frequently used, for reasons that will be clear
in a moment, is a sort of loan arrangement whereby the parent
company distributes funds to the subsidiaries and collects interest
on the amounts involved. The other method is that of increasing
the share participations by ENI in its subsidiary or affiliated companies. In the ENI balance sheet for April 30, 1962, the loan
financing account showed a balance of 149 billion lire and the
share participations account a balance of 118 billion; for the year
ending April 30, 1962, the profit and loss statement showed 15
billion lire in interest on the loan financing and only 6.3 billion
in dividends. Manifest here is a technique by which a government corporation can minimize the profits of its operating subsidiaries.

In 1962, the outstanding indebtedness of ENI in respect to long-,
medium- and short-term financing, exclusive of indebtedness to
suppliers, was 229 billion lire ($369,000,000), on which its annual

TABLE 2

ENI's Asset Growth

April 30	Net Profit (000,000)	Assets Total (000,000)	Assets Increase (000,000)	Source (000,000,000)	Application (000,000,000)
1954	2.340	43.907			
*1955	4.117	48.645	4.738		
*1956	4.158	52.484	3.839		
*1957	4.586	80.477	27.993	Long Term Borrowing 20.	Financing of Subsidiaries 27.
				Other Borrowing 3.	Bond Amortization 1.
1958	4.812	116.997	36.520	Long Term Borrowing 33.	Shareholdings 5.
					Financing of Subsidiaries 28.
					Bond Amortization 3.
1959	4.615	171.545	**54.548	Long Term Borrowing 54.	Financing of Subsidiaries 50.
					Bond Amortization 4.
1960	4.619	189.034	17.489	Bank Loans 19.5	Shareholdings 8.
					Financing of Subsidiaries 9.
1961	6.160	218.597	29.563	Long Term Borrowing 25.	Shareholdings 28.
1962	6.212	292.686	74.089	Long Term Borrowing 75.9	Shareholdings 43.2
					Financing of Subsidiaries 24.1

* Retained State's share of net profit for first three years.
** 14. To AGIP, 6. to pay off bank loan
   11. To AGIP Mineraria, 1.5 bank loans
   1.7 To SAIPEM
   1. To SNAM
   2.5 To AGIP Nucleare
   1. To IROM
   28.6 To SNAM (mostly Ravenna)
   ――――
   59.8

financing costs were slightly over thirteen billion lire. It will be noticed that the subsidiaries pay more for their ENI financing than ENI pays for the money with which it supplies them. It is obvious that ENI's indebtedness is excessively high. Ninety-five per cent of the indebtedness is bonded, and the principal and interest pertaining thereto are guaranteed by the government. Although the amount of bank loans outstanding was relatively low in 1962, these short- and medium-term loans have been used extensively by ENI in the past. Some of the affiliated companies have also obtained short- and medium-term money on their own accounts. At times, these amounts have been substantial; in 1959 for example, AGIP used almost one-half of its fourteen billion lire distribution of funds from the parent company to pay off its own bank loan. As a whole the ENI policy appears now to be that of using long-term funds to retire short-term obligations. In a very real sense, ENI has used a large portion of the new loans to pay off old loans and has been subjected to the charge that the company is only one loan ahead of its creditors.

Some Italians have been disturbed by the fact that ENI's manipulation of vast amounts of capital provides so little to the state in the form of a tangible return. In the April 30, 1962, Report, ENI revealed total sales of the ENI Group of approximately 406 billion lire and a net profit of only 6.2 billion, of which the government was entitled to about four billion lire. A member of the Chamber of Deputies, apparently disturbed by the incongruities between the huge debts and vast assets on one side and the relatively low sales and small profits on the other, wrote Mattei privately and asked for an explanation. The fog that surrounds ENI is beautifully illustrated by Mattei's polite response, which included the following statement:

"The fiscal returns shown in the balance sheets and subject to movable property tax have a complex techno-economic and legal structure whose relation to sales is indirect and is articulated and manifested in a system of administrative interrelations of costs and returns on operations in each individual economic business unit. Therefore I would put the question in these terms: if a private company shows a total activity of 361 billion lire in sales, articulated in an administrative system reproducing the coördinations of costs and returns and the fiscal-juridical structure of the operating budgets of the twenty-nine companies of the group and of ENI, should the payment of its direct taxes be in the proportion of about six and a half billion? The answer is decidedly yes. . . ."[18]

It would have been easier for Mattei to have repeated what he had said on so many other occasions: profits are not necessarily a useful measure of the performance of a public company. However, this would have left unanswered the question of the very low sales-assets ratio and might have raised issues involving the Po gas profits.

Buried under the vaster sums of recent years, the government's share of ENI's profits, which ENI was allowed to retain during the first three years of its existence, no longer seems very significant, though it provided a strategic eight billion lire at a time when even that small sum was badly needed.

ENI as an Antimonopolistic Force

If there was any single theme which dominated the public statements of ENI and Mattei, it was: "The ENI Group is an antimonopolistic force." This theme ran through almost all of the public relations efforts of the Ente; it permeated the annual reports; it was the refrain most frequently used by the sympathetic press; it was often the concluding phrase used even by Mattei's critics, who often wound up their attacks with a statement much like the following: ". . . but in spite of all these shortcomings, it must be said in Mattei's favor that he operates ENI as a great antimonopolistic force." This view is in keeping with postwar Italian political and economic traditions, which seem to demand that "monopolies" be blamed for most of Italy's economic problems. Where monopoly situations do in fact exist, and often where they do not exist but are believed to, the only solution ever seriously put forward is nationalization or direct state intervention. Consequently, the antimonopoly atmosphere overhangs any state participation in the economic sector. Although there was no petroleum monopoly nor any natural gas monopoly in Italy, and

in spite of the fact that ENI itself actually came into existence
as a monopoly in the Po Valley, the antimonopoly theme played
its part in the creation of ENI, and Mattei for many years made
constant use of the battle cry. Our interest here is in the question
of whether ENI really deserves to be called an "antimonopolistic
force." There does not appear to be very much evidence to support an affirmative answer, although there is strong evidence that
a negative answer would be closer to the truth.

Let us begin with a brief excerpt from ENI's annual report of
April 30, 1961:

"ENI has, in fixing the prices of its goods, always followed the
principle of enabling the Italian economy to have these goods
available at the lowest prices compatible with market conditions
and technological progress.

This trend has repeatedly taken a practical form in sectors of
strategic importance to the nation's economy where industry was
concentrated into the hands of a few to a very marked degree and
business was of a typically monopolistic nature.

The effects of ENI's massive intervention in the liquefied petroleum gas and nitrogenous and complex fertilizer sectors are
well-known. By forcing competitors to fall into line with the
Group's new rates, these measures have meant that money which
previously went to huge monopolistic receipts for the small
number of firms operating in these fields is now split among the
consumers.

ENI has more recently turned its attention to another far-reaching sector—with its reduction of gasoline and gas oil prices." [14]

Usually listed first in furtherance of ENI's antimonopoly reputation is the success with which ENI lowered the price of nitrogenous fertilizer in Italy. There is little question about the fact,
but there is some doubt as to how much credit ENI can take for
it, and of course it is impossible to discover whether ENI sells
its fertilizers at a loss. After ENI's large petrochemical installation at Ravenna went into operation, utilizing some of the Po
Valley gas, the price of the fertilizer produced in that plant was
sharply and dramatically reduced, but shortly thereafter the
price was raised to a point about midway between the old price

and the level of the first drastic reduction. Competitors, chiefly Montecatini, followed suit.

Methane is a major factor in the production of these fertilizers, so it is not difficult to understand what made it possible for ENI to reduce the prices of this product. The new prices are among the lowest in Europe and have been beneficial to Italian agriculture, but they are not so dramatic as the original reduction led everyone to believe they would be. The availability of natural gas in Italy undoubtedly had more to do with the lower prices of Italian fertilizers than did Mattei's appearance in the industry. Going the rounds in Rome in 1962 were persistent rumors that Mattei was seeking a price-fixing alliance with Montecatini,[16] Italy's chief producer of chemical fertilizers and the "monopoly" whose fertilizer prices ENI's operations were alleged to be directed against. If this proves to be true, Mattei's legend will be revised somewhat.

ENI's price for liquefied petroleum gas is not as low as one might expect of an organization with its substantial competitive advantages: a virtual monopoly of Italian sources of supply, competitors who must buy from ENI or import from abroad, and a reputation for antimonopolistic and antiforeign behavior. The effect of having competitive producers in the Po Valley might very well have been even lower prices of liquefied petroleum gas and other natural gas products. The gasoline, gas oil, and fuel oil price situations already have been examined and have been found to provide little evidence of antimonopolistic attitudes on the part of ENI, but to have strong political motivations in their backgrounds.

Offered in support of ENI's claim to the role of an antimonopolistic force is the following statement:

"ENI, by acquiring direct sources of crude oil supply, by making purchases abroad at the cheapest prices on the free market and by strengthening its own independent refining and marketing position, was able to force upon all the Italian and foreign enterprises operating in Italy a motor fuel price corresponding much better to the consumers' and expanding traffic requirements—an important factor for speeding up economic progress in countries where the standard of industrialization and living is already high." [16]

The phrase "cheapest prices on the free market" refers, of course, to the purchase of Russian oil. Mattei either believed, or vigorously alleged without believing, that the Russian price was competitive. In his bitter exchange with Montanelli, Mattei said that the high ("40 to 45 per cent") profit margins of the big international oil companies proved that their prices were not competitive, and concluded as follows:

"Elementary economics textbooks teach that a competitive price is one based on the cost of production plus a normal operating profit; hence it cannot include super-profits of the above dimensions. Therefore one would say that if the price of Russian oil is lower than that of the big companies, it certainly comes closer to being a competitive price." [17]

To Mattei, "monopoly" was just a public relations word used to condemn private companies and foreign companies without any reference to the nature or structure of the markets in which they operate. Mattei sought to obtain monopoly power wherever he went; he eliminated competition in exploration and production in the Po Valley; he accomplished much the same result in the rest of continental Italy and tried to do the same in Sicily; he demanded exclusive rights to import oil into countries where he built refineries. The antiforeign and nationalistic overtones of Mattei's policies with regard to monopoly are well demonstrated by the closing paragraph of the section of the 1961 annual report devoted to ENI "as an antimonopolistic force":

"ENI, through the direct part it plays in a fundamental sector of activity like oil clearly and openly based on relationships with new countries, and also through its contribution towards building up local industry by means of the firms it sets up to supply goods and services, so that its trademarks are becoming ever more widely known, is a driving force making Italy a country to reckon with on all the markets of the world." [18]

I think that it can be said in conclusion that, although ENI has tremendous potential to act as an antimonopolistic force, its performance under Mattei was not consistent, except in public relations, with antimonopoly as a professed policy.

ENI and the Mezzogiorno

We should not leave our discussion of ENI's economic performance without brief comments on the performance of ENI in Italy's perennial problem area, the Mezzogiorno. One of the great unsolved issues of Italy's modern history has been the burden which the poverty and backwardness of the South have placed on the remainder of the country. Even the most heroic efforts at a solution seem to terminate with this area relatively worse off than before. Lack of natural resources, a harsh and antiquated land tenure system, serious overpopulation, a low level of education and an historical disassociation from the rest of Italy make the problem an extremely difficult one. Migration to the North and to other European countries, some effective redistribution of the land, and general improvement in Italian economic conditions seem, at long last, to be making small headway. On the theory that only a vastly increased industrialization of the area can provide a long-range solution to the problem, Italian industry has been encouraged to build, expand, and invest in the south, but without many tangible results.

Although the Italian government has for many years controlled very large portions (about 50 per cent in 1962) of Italian industrial capacity, and consequently was in an excellent position to make a direct contribution to the task of industrializing the South, nothing but informal encouragement was given state-owned companies until 1957. In the Law of July 29, 1957, all state companies were required to invest at least 40 per cent of each year's new capital investment in the Mezzogiorno. As usual, no means of enforcement and no genuine audit were provided for in the law, so compliance is difficult to prove or disprove. The general supervision of the law was given to the Minister of State Participations (Ministro delle Partecipazioni Statali), who holds the portfolio

through which government control of state companies is expected
to be exercised. In addition to forwarding the annual financial
reports of the state-owned companies to Parliament, the Minister
also submits to Parliament programs (*relazioni*) for future investment and development for the companies under his alleged
control. These programs appear to be the means selected for
manifesting compliance with the Law of July 29, and do contain
specific reference to investments in the Mezzogiorno and to the
proportion which they bear to the total new investment.

As a source of information and as a measure of compliance with
the statute, these programs have several defects. Though submitted annually, they are not reports of past performance but are
predictions of investments to be made during the ensuing four-
year period, and the first such prediction was not made until 1960.
ENI has paid little attention to its investment program. Furthermore, the power pattern in the Italian government is such that
the strength lies with the state companies, not with the Minister.
The lack of any sort of effective audit forces the Minister, in
drafting his programs for the Parliament, to rely on the information provided to him by the companies.[19] Thus the programs do
not in any sense represent an independent appraisal of investment
in the South. ENI's estimates for the period 1960–1963 were extremely favorable, so far as investment in the South was concerned, showing that 65 per cent of the new capital would go to
that area. My feeling is that the figures represented real plans of
investment and were reasonably accurate presentations of the
plans, but are not being closely adhered to. The heavy investments
now being made in the petrochemical, thermoelectric, and refining
installations at Gela make up a large portion of the total, but the
Pignone Sud electronics plant at Bari, the natural gas developments at Ferrandina, the nuclear power plant near Anzio, and the
exploration activities in Basilicata and Sicily contribute significant
amounts. Prior to 1960, there is little question that ENI was preoccupied with the North and with overseas activities and was
giving little attention to the South, but the situation has now
changed radically.

Some Italian criticism of ENI in recent years has been based
on charges that Mattei was investing too much abroad and too
little at home, especially in the South. The charge with regard to
the South is clearly no longer true, and the general charge of too
little at home seems also to be unfounded on several grounds.
Mattei was convinced, I am sure, that Italy's own petroleum resources do not provide any long range solution to Italy's energy
needs. If petroleum is to be imported, how much better it would
be if it were to come from Italian controlled sources. One should
not forget Mattei's desperate search for "big oil" before his Po
gas fields fade out. Mattei, were it not for contradictory statements
made at other times and for other purposes, might have made a
strong argument that he was not investing enough abroad. Personally, I feel that a large portion of the Po Valley profits is now
going into the overseas search and, of course, does not appear on
the record. So far as published statements are concerned, the investment abroad is not large relative to ENI's total investment.
During the years 1959–1960, for example, the investment abroad
was six billion lire as compared with a total new investment of
seventy billion. Whether Mattei invested wisely abroad is another
question, dealt with elsewhere in this study, and one for which
there is as yet no definite answer.

In summary of this discussion of ENI's economic power and
performance, it can honestly be said that there is much on the
credit side of the picture, especially in connection with the discovery, development, and production of the Po natural gas, the
building of the pipelines, the introduction of modern methods and
techniques for marketing petroleum products, the economic resurrection of such depressed areas as Ravenna. Beyond these, the
performance is, at best, uncertain. The incredible proliferation
and diversification of activities has spread the economic and management resources of the Group very thin and undoubtedly has
diverted both kinds of resources from targets to which they might
have been more efficiently directed. It is not possible to point to
any particular operation as being unquestionably unsound or un-
profitable, but there is adequate evidence that among the many
companies making up the ENI Group, there is a substantial pro-

portion whose economic performance is unsatisfactory. The ratio of sales to assets is very unfavorable for petroleum companies or industrial companies in general, and even worse if we accept the view that the assets have been undervalued in an effort to conceal the extent and the use of the Po Valley profits.

CHAPTER 4

Apparatus of Power

Whereas the previous chapter was concerned primarily with economic power and performance, the present chapter will be devoted largely to specific manifestations of power and to the apparatus that facilitated the exercise of power. By studying the statutory mandate, which gave Mattei his warrant and his initial claim to legitimacy, and the art of public relations, which for Mattei was both a weapon of attack and a defensive rampart, we shall examine some of the ways in which the organization and management of ENI were designed and used to further the exercise of power. Space will be devoted also to a consideration of how Mattei employed the petroleum concession agreement in a treble power role to achieve economic, political, and personal ends. When these investigations have been accomplished, we shall be ready to isolate the power component in the ENI brew.

In striking contrast with other Italian public corporations was the way ENI was able to mobilize all of its resources and bring them to bear in support of a particular goal that might at a given moment become important. This was possible because Mattei planned it that way and because Mattei was always in control of his and ENI's images as well as of their actions. Adroitly using the statutory mandate as a base, ENI's centralized organization and the concession agreements as tools, and his own skillful public relations staff as scouts, light cavalry, and rear guard, Mattei was able to concentrate tremendous power on a narrow target. Other combinations of resources were employed from time to time, but dependence on public relations was a constant ingredient. The particular mix suggested in this chapter was one of the most important and most frequently used in the apparatus of power.

THE STATUTORY MANDATE

The mandate implicit in Article I of the Law of February 10, 1953, the statute by which ENI was brought into existence, was that ENI seek ways of alleviating Italy's acute shortage of petroleum energy. The article states that ENI "has the mission of promoting and taking initiative in the field of hydrocarbons and the natural vapors." [1] The history and background outlined in the previous chapter make it clear that the primary objective of the statute was to encourage the development of hydrocarbon resources in Italy, but the law does not specifically confine the scope of ENI's activities to this endeavor. Thus, the way was clearly open for exploration, production, purchase, and sale abroad.

There seems to be general agreement in Italy that the Po Valley, the area of ENI's exclusive rights, has been explored thoroughly and is in the process of being developed to the fullest possible extent. I do not believe that the condemnation of Mattei for his denial that there was any oil in the Po at the same time he was refusing to let anyone else look for it is justified. When a well is drilled, it cannot be forecast with accuracy whether oil, gas, or neither will be found. Mattei was apprehensive, no doubt, that someone searching for oil might find methane and break ENI's monopoly in what is still its most valuable product. Although the Valley once gave promise of containing deposits of liquid hydrocarbons, nothing of a substantial nature has ever been discovered. ENI is still drilling in the Po Valley and Mattei, until the last, was still denying that there was any oil to be found. It is very likely that the natural gas deposits are the extent of the Valley's petroleum resources.

Methane

Though the Po contains nothing more than methane, these resources are not to be minimized. The part that the Po gas has played in Italy's postwar "miracle" is inestimable. Without the Po the spectacular industrial growth of Northern Italy probably would have been a different story and might never have occurred. Although the price of methane is based on the price of imported fuel oil, methane is cleaner and more convenient to use and, in the case of Italy, does not require the expenditure of foreign exchange. Valuable as the Po Valley has been it cannot be looked to for any further miracles. Production has reached its peak and, even with good reservoir engineering and modern utilization techniques, probably can be maintained at its present annual rate of 6½ to 7 billion cubic meters for only another ten to twelve years. Some enemies of ENI have charged it with colossal waste in the Po Valley but there is very little in the way of evidence to support this charge. ENI has had outstanding foreign experts at its service and now has developed an excellent engineering staff of its own. There is little question now but that ENI's performance in the Po Valley, from a utilization point of view, has been good. Of course, the Po fields had been discovered and were well on their way toward full utilization before ENI came into existence, but for this purpose it is certainly permissible to tie Mattei's AGIP experience to that of ENI and conclude that in the Po area the public mandate has been carried out in a spectacular fashion.

In terms of methane, the performance has been universally satisfactory, though no other area of Italy has competed or is likely to compete with the unusual success in the Po. The natural gas discoveries in the Abruzzi, in Basilicata, and in Sicily probably are not going to trigger another miracle. Whereas the Po fields were only a short distance from major industrial centers whose factories were hungry for energy, the newly discovered fields are in the South and far from potential users. There was substantial opposition in the South of Italy to ENI's plans to transport the methane to existing industrial areas where it could be used, on the ground that local resources should be retained near their source so as to increase the benefits to the local residents. Plans have had to be modified, especially with regard to the Ferrandina field in Basilicata, and efforts are being made to bring industry to the gas rather than the gas to the industry. At this date, most of the

Ferrandina wells are capped, waiting for developments which are very slow in coming. Actually, Mattei may not have wanted the southern fields in operation because they would have destroyed his argument that the price of the Po gas must be kept high in order to avoid any further increase in the advantages the North enjoys over the South. The record of discovery of methane has been good, but utilization, outside the Po Valley, is proceeding very slowly. All things considered, however, I think that it can safely be said that in methane ENI has effectively carried out its statutory mandate.

Oil

Except for natural gas, ENI's performance in petroleum is spectacular only in terms of diplomacy and politics. ENI's figures on its drilling operations in Italy during 1960 (320,348.8 meters drilled and 161 wells completed) are rather impressive, when viewed alone, but in comparison with explorations in other countries are niggardly. More wells were drilled on the island of Trinidad than ENI drilled in all of Italy. In the United States, during the same year, 46,778 wells were completed. Whether the relatively low level of exploration activity by ENI in Italy is a contributing factor in the low level of discoveries cannot be said with certainty. Because competitive exploration has been almost completely eliminated from Italy, it is difficult to make any comparisons, but ENI has had a free hand in the Po Valley since 1949, in effect, and in Italy as a whole (outside Sicily) since 1957, with few results. That there is no oil to be found in Italy is a strong possibility, but the extent of ENI drilling activity has been insufficient so far to prove this conclusively, and no one else is drilling. ENI's total oil production in Italy and Sicily in 1961 was 556,698 tons. Except for trickles here and there, the remainder of Italy's slightly more than two-million-ton total production came from the Gulf field at Ragusa. ENI's production will increase as facilities for handling the poor quality Gela crude are completed. However, I was unable to find anyone, outside ENI, who could suggest any possible economic basis on which ENI could refine or use all of the three million tons of Gela crude per year that Mattei claimed to be

striving toward. A likely possibility still is that a major portion
of the Gela facilities will never be used for Gela crude, but are
really intended for as-yet-undiscovered sources abroad.

The proportion of Italian petroleum needs that must be met by
imports has been increasing over the last several years, as would,
of course, be inevitable if domestic production had reached its
peak. Of the petroleum that must be imported each year, ENI's
sources abroad provide a small proportion. Egypt makes available
not more than one million tons a year, and delivery is uncertain;
the present discoveries in Iran may, before long, provide up to
two million tons; other sources outside of Italy now appear to
be good for a maximum of one million a year for the next few
years. ENI, then, can provide from its own foreign fields not more
than four million tons of Italy's present, and rapidly growing,
petroleum imports of twenty million tons a year. As a matter of
fact, ENI cannot even supply its own petroleum needs, and has
refining capacity far in excess of its ability to produce its own oil.
These are the hard facts that brought about ENI's agreement with
the USSR, under which ENI in 1962 obtained 38 per cent of its
own needs.

Mattei's success in negotiating concession agreements, particularly with Arab countries, was remarkable, though a good
deal of that success was due not to his skill but to his seemingly
attractive terms, and to the fact that granting concessions to
Mattei fitted in with certain Arab goals. Although Mattei described his terms as the only fair way to deal with the countries
under whose soil the oil was hoped to repose, it seems rather obvious that the terms were worked out as an inducement, not as a
gift. Many of the arrangements are not very beneficial to ENI or
to Italy, and none of them has yet resulted in large quantities of
oil. In liquid petroleum, Mattei did not do much to improve
Italy's drain of foreign exchange. It is very likely that Italy will
always have to depend on sources abroad for most of its petroleum needs, and this circumstance cannot be laid at ENI's door,
but ENI so far has done precious little to provide Italian-con-
trolled sources of foreign oil. Perhaps Mattei spread his efforts
too thin in his foreign explorations, and perhaps he was on oc-

casion penny-wise and pound-foolish in picking his concessions, but until time has had more to say on the matter, it may be best not to condemn too quickly or too much. ENI has been lucky in the past, and there is no reason to believe that luck will desert the Ente now; but an industrial enterprise of the size and importance of ENI would seem to be a bit more secure were its future not quite so dependent on luck.

The pricing of ENI's products is discussed in greater detail elsewhere. Insofar as prices are relevant to an appraisal of performance under the statutory mandate, it can be said that the price of the Po natural gas was tied to the price of competitive fuel oil and is probably two or three times the cost of extracting and delivering the gas. This price is not excessive, in absolute terms, and ENI could sell more gas than it presently produces. Furthermore, a good argument could be made, until recently, for avoiding any further additions to the already long list of disparities between the North of Italy and the Mezzogiorno. The price of AGIP gasoline has several times been slightly reduced, but these reductions appear to have been made primarily for political purposes, e.g., the Russian oil contract, as has been stated. For at least two more reasons, little significance can be attached to AGIP's reduction in gasoline prices: in the first place, more than 70 per cent of the price of gasoline in Italy is made up of taxes; in the second place, the nontax portion of the price is very low to start with, and there is evidence to support the conclusion that neither AGIP nor its competitors is doing better than breaking even on sales of gasoline. ENI public relations make much of the fact that gasoline is cheaper in Italy than it is in the United States—*ignoring taxes*, though this qualification is sometimes omitted.

Scope of the Mandate

Once we leave the hydrocarbons themselves, it is even more difficult to assess ENI's performance under its statutory mandate. "Field of hydrocarbons," as the scope of ENI's activities is set forth in the enabling statute, can without undue strain be interpreted to include pipelines, motels, and petrochemical activities. To bring electronics, publishing, and knitting into the scope takes more effort. The problem, however, is not just a matter of interpreting the language of the statute. It is crystal clear by now that Mattei saw his mandate as being much broader than any interpretation of language could possibly support. Mattei pointed to the Program Report,[2] which the Minister of State Participations submitted to the Parliament in 1961, for the working definition of his mandate. Of course, Mattei was operating under this definition years before the new Ministry of State Participations was even dreamed of, and, as is pointed out elsewhere in this study, Mattei probably wrote the Program Report. The Report sets forth three purposes or objectives for state intervention in Italy's economic affairs: 1) "to achieve certain basic requirements of an economic and social nature and, more specifically, to secure that development of services without which it seems impossible to attain a higher standard of living or take more far-reaching action to promote new productive enterprises"; 2) "the development of certain sectors of activity should not be decided by taking into account current market situations or the prospects of making quick profits alone, but should rather be directed towards achieving a higher long-term rate of growth and adjusted to fit the need for balanced progress in the nation's economic affairs"; and 3) "minimization of the handicaps that may derive from the monopolistic policy of certain combines."

In Italian economic, political, and legal theory, these three "objectives" were once the "grounds" on which state intervention in the private sector of the economy might be justified. Whatever else they may have become, they were the principles by which Mattei conducted his operations. Mattei found here all the justification he needed for extending ENI's activities to any portion of the Italian economy, for his strong antiprivate enterprise statements and conduct, and for his bestowing on ENI the benediction: "antimonopolistic force." If these objectives really constituted his mandate, they would seem to have been coextensive with the constitutional mandate of the Italian government, and to appraise them would be far outside the scope of this brief study. If they are not, and if ENI's mandate is limited to activities somehow related to the hydrocarbons, a few comments can be made.

From unaudited financial statements, it is impossible to determine whether any of the Mattei ventures outside petroleum are successful. Without doubt, some are and some are not. Even with the best of financial information available, an appraisal still would be handicapped by the twin questions of whether the activity could be justified under the statutory mandate and of what might be the underlying reason for venturing into that activity. Mattei's reasons were often more political or personal than economic, but were never so expressed. To justify a woolen knitting mill in the Veneto (Lanerossi) as a potential market for synthetic fibers to be produced in the future at a natural gas field in Basilicata leaves some questions unanswered, and one is inclined to accept the more Machiavellian objectives attributed to Mattei by the sceptics. In summary, little more can be said about Mattei's nonpetroleum activities than this: some seem to be outside all but the broadest constructions of the ENI statute; some were entered for reasons other than economic advantage or national interest; and none really can be deeply penetrated through the veil of protective financial statements.

ORGANIZATION AND MANAGEMENT

The quality of ENI's organization and management cannot be read in its financial statements, as we have already discovered, and cannot be ascertained from the reputation built, in large part, by the Ente's own public relations activities. It is possible, however, to measure certain aspects of the organization and its management against known standards in Italy and abroad in order to obtain some help in determining whether ENI can be expected to operate efficiently and effectively within its spheres of activity. Mattei always devoted considerable attention to the organization of the ENI Group and to the routines and procedures by which, on all levels, its operations were carried on.

On paper, and to a remarkable extent in practice also, the organization of the entire ENI complex reflects the fact that, early in the life of ENI, Mattei employed the services of one of the best American management consulting firms, listened to its advice, and hired away one of its best experts to head up his Management Engineering (Tecnico Direzione) Section, which is responsible for organization planning, systems planning, and organization policies and procedures. The result is that any American familiar with the principles and policies underlying an effective organization would be able to find his way around ENI with no great difficulty. There are some things about the framework of the ENI organization that would surprise the American observer, and many aspects of the actual practice which would be startling, but most of these variations result from differences in the Italian environment and not from any failure to adopt good administrative principles.

There is an exception to these conclusions, however, and it is found at the very top of the organization, though its effects permeate the entire structure. In practice, the control of the ENI Group is incredibly concentrated in the hands of its president and yet consists of a multiplicity of operating companies established for political or legal, rather than economic or organizational, purposes.

Legal Structure

Thorough examination of the Italian public corporation and of ENI's own legal structure are beyond the scope of this study, but some attention must be given to these topics in order to set the stage for the evaluation of ENI's organization and management. The intervention of the Italian state in the nation's economic affairs takes a number of different forms. The three most common are the following: 1) Direct intervention through a government department or ministry. The Post Office Department in the United States provides an illustrative parallel. The budget of the activity is part of the government's own budget; the activity has no legal personality of its own; the activity is regulated almost entirely by public law. 2) Intervention by government purchase of shares in existing corporations or joint stock companies. The purchase may be of a majority or of less than a majority of the shares, in which case private shareholders retain an interest in the activity, or of all the outstanding shares. The budget of the company is not associated with the budget of the government; the company has its own distinct legal personality; its affairs are largely a matter of private law; and it tends to preserve its character as a private company. 3) Intervention through what are called in Italy "economic public corporations" (*enti pubblici economici*), government-owned corporations. The company is endowed by the state with distinct legal personality for the purpose of carrying on the functions outlined in the statute which created it; its budget is independent of the government's budget, except insofar as the government may make donations of capital or receive the profits of the operation; activities are regulated primarily under rules of private law. The lines among the three forms are not well delineated in Italian law.

ENI, of course, falls into the third category. The Ente was brought into existence by the Law of February 10, 1953, and was endowed with legal personality. Because each one of the economic public corporations is created by its own statute, there is considerable variation among them, but elements of the basic pattern remain much the same, and some problems are common to all. For example, there has been controversy in the past as to whether the status of employees of economic public corporations was such as to be controlled by public law and subject to the jurisdiction of the *Consiglio di Stato*, the highest administrative court, or by private law and subject to the jurisdiction of the *Corte di Cassazione*, the highest civil court. The ENI statute avoided this difficulty by stating expressly, in Article 18, that the relationship between the company and its employees was to be controlled by private law.

Although the establishment of the economic public corporations is by special act of Parliament and the companies are wholly government owned, they are still modeled on the private stock company or corporation, except that shareholders' meetings are not necessary. The most important administrative organ in these companies is the board of directors (*consiglio d'amministrazione*), charged with general supervision of the company; where the board of directors is large, the company usually is also provided with an executive committee (*giunta esecutiva*). In addition, there is a president (*presidente*), who may be the chief executive officer with real authority, as in ENI, or simply a figurehead or an honorary officeholder; if the company also has a director general (*direttore generale*), the president's function is likely to be relatively unimportant. ENI had no director general during Mattei's term, but many of its subsidiary companies did; in the case of the subsidiaries, the relative importance of the two offices could easily be determined by looking to see which one was occupied by Mattei.[3] In addition to these groups and offices is the board of auditors (*collegio sindacale*), which is intended, even in Italian private companies, to act in an auditing and supervisory capacity over the accounts and over other financial activities of the company. Article 15 of the ENI statute also provides for a "delegate" from the Court of Accounts (*Corte dei Conti*) to assist at meetings of the board of directors and of the board of auditors; the Court of Accounts was created by Article 100 of the Italian Constitution of 1948 for the purpose of auditing governmental operations. The "delegate" from the Court of Accounts is empowered to denounce before Parliament any irregularities or violations by the company in which he sits.

The various officers and board members are appointed by the government. The president, vice-president, and the members of the board of directors and executive committee, all of whom hold office for three-year terms, are named by the president of the Council of Ministers on nominations made by the Ministers of the Treasury, Industry and Commerce, and State Participations. The Board of Directors of ENI is required, by law, to include among its number an employee of the company; the board also contains representatives of various ministries, the president, vice-president, and five "experts." Members of the Board of Auditors are appointed by certain ministers, and must include representatives from the Government Accounting Office and from specified ministries and two "professional members," chosen from among the legal, accounting, and academic professions. The Court of Accounts selects its own delegate.[4]

An appropriate *caveat* at this point takes the same form it would take if this study were devoted to a large American private corporation rather than to an Italian public company. ENI's legal form of organization, described in the paragraphs above, bears little resemblance to the actual form. On paper, ENI looks much like any other Italian public or private corporation, but there the resemblance ceases. Any similarity between the legal form and the actual form is purely coincidental. The simple fact is that Enrico Mattei controlled every major aspect of the ENI Group, not because of any particular title he held or board or committee he controlled, but because he was Enrico Mattei. The Board of Directors, the Executive Committee, and the Board of Auditors had no substantive function and met only in order to comply with the barest minimum of legal requirements. Their only requirement was to put the official stamp of approval on what Mattei had already done or decided to do and to sign the various official statements and reports to the government. Nothing more can be said for the delegate from the Court of Accounts. There is no need to make a detailed analysis of the purported functions of the various administrative organs required by law; little of what might be told would have application to ENI. Changes since Mattei's death cannot yet be satisfactorily evaluated.

Financing of Italian public economic companies is characterized by an original donation from the state, in the form of cash or property, and in preferred access to the various sources of credit. Bonds and other forms of borrowing are guaranteed by the government, with respect to both interest and principal, and are exempt from public charges and taxes, both present and future.[5] A few of the companies, including ENI, are made free of taxes, except for a nominal amount on the capitalization.[6] Profits, if any, are remitted to the state, though customarily a portion may be retained for research and training and for setting up a reserve fund. In the case of ENI, the statute provides that 65 per cent of the profits goes to the Treasury, while 20 per cent is held by the Ente for allocation to an "ordinary reserve fund" and 15 per cent is retained for research and training in the energy sector of the economy.[7] However, the fact that the accounts of the Ente are wholly unaudited either by the government or by an independent agency, means that the announced profit figures are of little significance as a guide to operational success or efficiency of organization.[8]

Organization of the ENI Group

The one-man control of the ENI Group by Enrico Mattei cannot be used immediately as evidence that the Group is necessarily heir to all the ills commonly associated with such heavily centralized operations. Actually, an efficient organization was a prerequisite to Mattei's being able to control such a large complex of companies engaged in activities ranging all the way from newspapers to rubber. The organization of ENI was a key factor in Mattei's power and in the effectiveness with which it could be exercised. The continued rapid growth and the still heavy reliance placed on the Po Valley gas, however, are putting ever increasing pressure on his organization. In the study of the organization of ENI, there is no practical way to avoid the identification of the company with Mattei. In general, what was good or bad about Mattei is also good or bad about the ENI Group. The effects of his personality are found everywhere.

Charts A and B show the basic organization of the ENI Group. ENI itself is essentially an administrative and holding company and engages in no operational activity. Under its direct control are the five major operating companies and under them more than seventy-five others. AGIP Mineraria is engaged in exploration for and production of hydrocarbons all over the world and operates both directly and through approximately twenty subsidiaries or affiliated companies. AGIP is a marketing company whose trademarks, the six-legged dog and the cat with a gas jet in its tail, are becoming well-known all over the world. AGIP also operates through a host of subsidiary and affiliated companies. AGIP Nucleare is engaged in nuclear research and will operate the nuclear power plant now nearing completion near Anzio. Azienda Nazionale Idrogenazione Combustibili (ANIC) is the refining and petrochemical company and operates the massive industrial complex at Ravenna. Società Nazionale Metanodotti (SNAM) is the only one of the five "headgroup" companies that cannot be described in a sentence, and I am not at all sure that it can be

CHART A

GRUPPO ENI *

AGIP MINERARIA **

Exploration for and production of hydrocarbons (Italy, Egypt, Iran, Somalia, Morocco, Libya, and elsewhere)

SNAM **

Nuovo Pignone (Makes drilling equipment, pumps, prefabricated gas stations, instruments, etc.; also sells outside.)

SNAM Progetti Planning and design

SAIPEM Domestic and foreign construction and contracting

Transportation subsidiaries (including pipeline)

AGIP & AFFILIATES

Distribution (Italy, Germany, Austria, Switzerland, England, Somalia, Morocco Libya, Tunisia, Eritrea, Ghana, Sudan, and elsewhere)

ANIC **

Refining and Petrochemicals

AGIP NUCLEARE **

Nuclear power stations and research

* As of 1962.

** All reported through Girotti in Operations and Control, except AGIP which reported directly to Mattei. (See Chart C.)

CHART B
Affiliated Companies in the ENI Group (April 30, 1962)

AGIP MINERARIA	AGIP

MINER. SICILIA ORIENTALE	IDROBITUME ZABBAN	AGIP Ltd. (Great Britain)
RAVENNATE METANO	IROM	AGIP CASABLANCA (Morocco)
SAMPOC	SEMI	AGIP Ltd. (Kenya - Uganda - Tanganyika)
SAMPOR	SERAM	AGIP NIGERIA
SOIS	STEI	AGIP SOMALIA
SOMICEM	AGIP A. G. (Austria)	AGIP SUDAN
SOMIS	AGIP A. G. (West Germany)	AGIP S. A. (Switzerland)
VULCANO	AGIP ARGENTINA	AGIP TOGO
AGIP MINERARIA SUDAN	AGIP CAMERUN	AGIP TUNISI (Tunisia)
CORI (Libya)	AGIP COSTA D'AVORIO	GAZ ORIENT (Lebanon)
IEOC (Egypt)	AGIP DAHOMEY	OLYMPIAGAS (Greece)
COPE (Egypt)	AGIP GHANA	PETROLIBIA (Libya)
MINERARIA SOMALA (Somalia)	AGIP GIBUTI	ASSEIL (Libya)
SIRIP (Iran)	AGIP LIBERIA	
SITEP (Tunisia)		
SOMIP (Morocco)		

SNAM	ANIC	AGIP NUCLEARE

AZ. METANODOTTI PADANI	ANIC GELA	SIMEA
LABORATORI RIUNITI	CHIMICA RAVENNA	SINTEREL
METANO CITTÀ	LANEROSSI	SOMIREN
SAIPEM	PHILLIPS CARBON BLACK ITALIANA	
SIM	SALPO	
SNAM PROGETTI	SAPIR	
AGIP U.S.A.	SIPO	
OLEODOTTO DEL RENO (Switzerland)	STANIC	
OLEODOTTO DEL RODANO (Switzerland)	GHAIP (Ghana)	
SÜDPETROL (West Germany)	SAMIR (Morocco)	
ERDÖLRAFFINERIE INGOLSTADT A. G.	STIR (Tunisia)	

NUOVO PIGNONE		SOFID
PIGNONE SUD		SEGISA
FUCINE MERIDIONALI		STIEM

adequately described in a paragraph, page, or chapter. In many ways, it is the most interesting of ENI's major companies and, of them all, was the one least subject to day by day intervention by Mattei. Most of SNAM's activities during Mattei's lifetime were left in the hands of Ingegnere Girotti, the "Number Two" man in the ENI hierarchy (if "Two" can be said to describe the very wide gap in power and authority between "One" and "Two"). SNAM handles the transportation end of the business, including oil tankers and pipelines, but, beyond that, controls three of the most important ENI operating companies: Nuovo Pignone, SNAM Progetti, and SAIPEM (Società Azionaria Italiana Perforazioni e Montaggi). Nuovo Pignone was a semidefunct manufacturer of heavy machinery in Florence and on the verge of liquidation when Mattei bought it. Apparently the company now operates profitably, making drilling equipment, pumps, machinery, prefabricated service stations, instruments, and other metal products. A subsidiary, Pignone Sud, is now building a plant in Bari for the manufacture of metering and control equipment. SNAM Progetti is a planning and design organization which does work for other parts of the ENI Group and also for outside firms. SAIPEM is one of the world's largest construction and engineering firms and has built or is building, in Italy and abroad, highways, dams, nuclear power plants, refineries, pipelines, and a wide variety of mills, factories, and other industrial establishments.

ENI itself is divided into four divisions: Planning, Public Relations, Operations and Control, and New Industrial Initiatives Abroad. (See Chart C.) Nominally, a man of something like vice-presidential rank heads up each one of these divisions, but Mattei's own ideas often interfered with the organization chart. For example, Mattei managed the Public Relations division himself, and, although four of the five major operating companies reported to Girotti, who headed up the operations and control division, AGIP by-passed Girotti and reported directly to Mattei.

If one ignores the peculiarities imposed on the organization by Mattei's own wishes and conduct, the organization of ENI makes quite a lot of sense. ENI acts as a sort of management company, supervising the activities of the entire group of companies through

ENI ADMINISTRATION *

(1) PLANNING

(a) Market Research
(b) Servizio Tecnico; Considers project in which might invest money
(c) Servizio Programmazione; Investment planning and priorities—what it will cost
(d) Servizio Finanziario; Treasurer's function—where to get the money

(2) PUBLIC RELATIONS

(a) Press Office
(b) Speeches, booklets, etc.
(c) Advertising and publications
(d) Protocol office (greet visiting dignitaries, launch ships, etc.)
(e) Social studies; (studies effect on the community of price or product changes, new plants, etc.)
(f) Economics
(g) Government relations; (among other things, watches legislation closely for possible effects on ENI)

(3) OPERATIONS AND CONTROL

AGIP

| SNAM | AGIP N. |
| ANIC | AGIP M. |

Staff Organization for Operations

Comptroller   Coördinator of Staff

(a) Administration
(b) Personnel
(c) Management Engineering
   (i) Organization planning (including job description and evaluation)
   (ii) Policy and procedure
   (iii) Systems planning
   (iv) Operations Research
(d) Materials (controls and purchasing)
(Each of these is represented in each operating company)

(4) NEW INDUSTRIAL INITIATIVES ABROAD

E.g.—Oil concessions and refinery in Tunisia

* As of 1962.

the operations and control division and the five major subsidiaries. Most of the more important staff functions, planning, public relations, job evaluation, and purchasing, for example, are handled directly by ENI or are tightly controlled by the parent company. The ENI staff is forward-looking, capable, and for the most part well trained in modern management techniques. Considerable use is made of computers, accounting machinery, modern systems analysis, and operations research, and ENI has one of the best management training programs in Europe. The company maintains an excellent economic studies section, though it is somewhat surprising to find this section in the public relations division. The explanation is simply that "Mattei wanted it there." Mattei's very broad interpretation of "public relations" would have justified the location within the public relations division of almost any conceivable activity. The organization of the ENI Group is not haphazard but reflects Mattei's interest in organizational matters and his appreciation of the importance to him of an effective operational setup.

Under Mattei, the multiple operating units were not a serious organizational problem. Most of the units were required by the exigencies of politics or law and could not easily have been avoided. What is more important, however, is the fact that to a large extent their existence was more a matter of form than of substance, and they were tightly controlled by their parent companies or by the head office. However, they do present several vexing problems to Mattei's successors. These men are inheriting a situation they did not create and with which they do not, of course, have the intimate, broad-gauge familiarity of the man who built the organization.

The heavy centralization of ENI's management is certainly the salient fact about the whole organization. A glance at Table 3 will further emphasize this concentration of authority under Mattei. During the winter of 1961–62, the new refinery in Rabat, Morocco (built by ENI and jointly owned by ENI and the government of Morocco), was completed and dedicated. The dedication ceremony was attended by many members of the Italian cabinet, including the Prime Minister, Fanfani, and, of course, was

TABLE 3

ENRICO MATTEI'S OFFICIAL POSITIONS IN THE
MAJOR COMPANIES OF THE ENI GROUP
(1962)

ENI	President
AGIP Mineraria	President
SNAM	President
AGIP	Director General
ANIC	President
STANIC	President
AGIP Nucleare	President

to be attended by Mattei. Just before Mattei's takeoff from Rome in his executive jet, it was discovered that the plane had been sabotaged. (This was blamed on the Algerian OAS, angered because Mattei, long before the independence of Algeria seemed likely, was alleged to have negotiated with the Algerian FLN for postindependence oil rights.) This near miss on Mattei's life emphasized the importance of a question that had frequently been asked of ENI executives, government officials, professors, and newspapermen. What would happen to ENI if Mattei should suddenly be removed from the scene? With some variation in degree, the same answer was heard everywhere. ENI would sooner or later collapse, or perhaps disintegrate into its many component parts.

The sad fact is that in 1962 there was no one in the organization who could possibly have taken Mattei's place. The one real possibility, Eugenio Cefis, left the company on January 1, 1962, to return to his own business interests. However, Cefis was brought back to ENI as vice-president after Mattei's death and may be slated to replace Professor Boldrini, an elderly man, who was named to the presidency. Cefis possesses some of Mattei's vitality, originality, and flair for the broader aspects of top management, but lacks the political power, national reputation, public relations skill, and intimate knowledge of the Ente that were the cornerstones of Mattei's success. Girotti is an excellent operations man but does not have the background, personality, and, probably, the desire for the top job. Boldrini, who was named by the government to replace Mattei, is well past his prime at the age of seventy-two and has had almost nothing to do with the actual management of the ENI Group, although he has carried the title of vice-president of ENI since 1953 and was president of AGIP before that. Almost any other position in the vast complex of ENI companies could probably be filled from among the supply of good-quality managers and technicians. But to replace Mattei, there was no crown prince, no regent, nor even a healthy usurper. Only time will tell what the government's plans are for ENI and whether anyone can hold ENI together as more than a loose association of companies. To accomplish even the latter may prove to be a major achievement.

Most of the Italian government's extensive participation in the economic sector of society is carried on through two large public companies: ENI and Istituto per la Ricostruzione Industriale (IRI). The latter dates back to the Mussolini days, is approximately twice the size of ENI, and has well over one hundred subsidiary and affiliated companies engaged in everything from shipping and aircraft to steel, automobiles (Alfa Romeo), and banking. Unlike ENI, however, IRI is less of a "business firm" and more of a "government bureau" engaged in supervising business firms. Its organization is decentralized, loose and amorphous; it lacks the political power that Mattei gave to ENI and hence is much more subject to government constraint and influence. Some of its subdivisions operate efficiently and effectively, but there is tremendous variation from one to another. True, the present managers of IRI inherited a situation they did not themselves create, whereas Mattei built ENI, in effect, from scratch; but the two are as different as day is from night. When an Italian thinks of AGIP or ANIC or SAIPEM, he thinks of Mattei and ENI, but when an Italian thinks of Finsider or the Banco di Roma or Alfa Romeo, he thinks neither of IRI nor of a president whose name he probably has never heard. It seems possible that without Mattei ENI may disintegrate as a unit and become another IRI, assuming, of course, that a financial crisis does not cause something much worse than disintegration.

Two or three men have held all of the top executive positions in the entire ENI Group. In large part, this is because of Mattei's own dominant position, but part of the blame must be placed on a facet of the Italian national character, discussed in greater detail elsewhere. An Anglo-Saxon businessman trusts his employees and associates until he has cause not to; an Italian executive usually does not trust associates and employees until they have been tested over a considerable period of time. Where an American would appoint someone to fill a vacated position of trust an Italian would do the work himself until he found someone who had proven himself trustworthy. The Italian attitude has had many stultifying effects upon management, not the least of which is the tendency to narrow the executive class, even to keeping it within a single family, and the tendency toward heavily centralized management. ENI, like most Italian companies, suffers from these effects.

Before we leave the subject of organization and management, it should be pointed out that there is one problem of Italian mores which ENI seems successfully to have overcome, namely, the obligation to employ the relatives, friends, and political creditors of government officials. Even many private firms are affected by this custom, but ENI has successfully avoided it. From the very beginning Mattei refused this sort of request and in later years was rarely bothered. It was told me on good authority that Mattei weakened only twice on this score, both times on requests from officials of cabinet rank. One of these appointees, however, turned out to be extremely capable and now occupies a high and responsible position in the ENI organization. On a similar count, however, ENI does not do so well. The organization still seems to follow the Italian custom of avoiding the outright discharge of an unsatisfactory employee.

Manager Shortage

ENI has been badly handicapped by the critical shortage of managers that has made itself evident throughout Italian industry. Many factors have contributed to the shortage, including Italy's late development as an industrial economy; but the most important factors today are, unfortunately, ones that are not being solved very rapidly. One of these is certainly the educational system, which culminates in a university graduate with a magnificent classical training but neither the desire nor the ability to earn a living at anything very practical. Even the engineers graduate with excellent theoretical knowledge but with little practical knowledge which they might use to design a refinery, a manufacturing process, or a bridge. Employers must put up with a long unproductive period during which a new man receives his training. Much of ENI's training program is devoted to turning "engineers" into petroleum or refinery or civil engineers. Count Sforza called attention to this educational problem years ago and listed it as one of Italy's two most deadly enemies, along with nationalistic vanity. Its ramifications for general management are much more serious than they are for technical management. University graduates look down on commercial careers and have little background with which to undertake them. The result often is that either engineers move into these jobs (although there are plenty of technical jobs left undone, and engineers do not always themselves possess the proper training or attitude for top management) or those without university educations are trained for the jobs. In recent years Italy appears to have developed a shortage of engineers who are willing to leave safe engineering jobs for the uncertainties and responsibilities of general management.

Another and related cause of the manager shortage in Italy is the very narrow way in which the term "manager" is defined in that country. The American terminology of "middle managers," "top managers," "junior executives," is almost unheard of in Italy. The "managers" or "executives" in even the largest Italian firms consist of the top man and perhaps two or three others. Regardless of title or function, everyone else is looked upon as an employee or clerk whose job is to take orders from the managers. The problems of trust and delegation of authority, mentioned above, aggravate the manager problem, and capable young men are reluctant to enter the business world where they cannot look forward to "manager" status for thirty or forty years, if ever. ENI invests large sums in training managers and still cannot meet all of its own demands. Many of its best young men are bid away by other firms, especially private ones. Mattei's grandiose schemes and rapid expansion stretched the available talent to the utmost. Many of the objections from within ENI to Mattei's acquisition of the Lanerossi knitting firm were based on this problem. Nobody in ENI knows much about knitting, but some bright young men are being detached from other activities where they are badly needed in order to learn about it.

Under the circumstances, the organization and management of the ENI Group are better than could be expected. There are elements of real ingenuity, ability, and strength. There is great loyalty to the company and there was great personal loyalty to Mattei. The question is whether these positive factors can balance out or overcome the difficulties and frustrations of the environment in which they must operate. For Mattei's purposes, however, and for the effective exercise of his power, the organization of the ENI Group was admirably designed and capably employed.

CONCESSION AGREEMENTS

To an international oil company the concession agreement it makes with the host country is much like the franchise granted to a public utility. Negotiation and consummation of the agreement are necessary before oil can be searched for, discovered, produced, or carried away. Like the more familiar "franchise," it is often intensely competed for by a number of rival companies but, once granted, usually carries an exclusive privilege in a specified geographical area for a considerable period of time. Some of the major concessions were preceded by years of negotiating, wheedling, bribing, stringpulling, pressuring, entertaining, and politicking on a local, national, and international level. Although most of the major companies operating in the Middle East are or purport to be private companies (a policy reinforced by the edict of the Arab League, January, 1956, against participation by foreign governments in companies holding concessions from members of the League),[9] it is not unusual for pressures to be brought to bear by governments and on the very highest governmental levels. The term "concession agreement" has no clear-cut technical or legal meaning but is simply the most common term used to describe the arrangements worked out between the host country and the oil company. The word "concession" has some overtones of rights extracted by superior power, and its use often is avoided for that reason. Many of the agreements bear no title at all. The agreement between the Iran Consortium and the government of Iran is referred to by its parties as "an agreement without a name."

The details of the agreements vary considerably from place to place and from time to time, but all conform to certain basic patterns. All contain descriptions of the activities which the oil company is to carry on, delineation of the area of operation within the country, the amount and method of payment of the royalties, the duration of the agreement and an arbitration clause. In addition to these clauses, most of the agreements also contain provisions reflecting the major economic role to be played by the company in the host country: employment and training of local labor; contributions toward costs of education, social welfare, roads, health, water supplies, and other public services; participation by the government in the management; bonus and dead rent payments; and annual reports of operations.[10]

During the last quarter-century, even some of the details of the concession agreements have tended toward uniformity. The primary reason for this was the abrupt removal by World War II of German, Italian, and Japanese companies from the international oil industry; along with them went most of the economically irrational conduct. Predictable oligopolistic behavior began to set the pattern for the industry, with a measure of overt and covert coöperation to help it along. All the participants came from similar cultural and economic backgrounds, and their codes of "gentlemanly" conduct were essentially the same. Here originated the international petroleum "club," whose members understood each other and saw only futility and chaos in too vigorous open competition for the favors of present or potential host countries. The royalty clause was the most tempting target for competitive conduct, but even there remarkable restraint was shown. The famous 50-50 agreement came into common use in Venezuela in the 1940's as that country pressed for a better deal in its oil concessions, but did not appear in the Middle East until 1950 when the Arabian American Oil Company introduced it in the concession agreement with Saudi Arabia. This act upset the "club" somewhat, not so much because of the 50-50 agreement, which certainly could not be said to have been unexpected, but because of the lack of advance notice of its actual use in the Middle East. By 1952, the 50-50 pattern was almost universal in the Middle East, and remains so today.

Enter Mattei—Iran

Onto this stage walked Enrico Mattei. Revenge for the alleged 1954 rebuff by the Iran Consortium appears to have become one of the guiding principles of his life. He lacked knowledge and skill in international petroleum affairs, but he also lacked the restraining influences of "club" rules, and he had a "cause." The Consortium fought him vigorously and apparently came very close to persuading the Shah of Iran not to grant any concession to ENI, but clever public relations by Mattei and attractive concession terms overcame the Consortium's arguments that ENI was inexperienced in exploration matters and lacked the refining capacity and the markets necessary for proper exploitation of any oil that might be found. ENI obtained substantial rights in the new Qum field in the Zagros Mountains, offshore and not a stone's throw from the Consortium's main refinery at Abadan, and also offshore near the Pakistan border. An American company (Pan-American, a subsidiary of Standard of Indiana) and a Canadian company (Sapphire) rode in on Mattei's coattails.

The ENI concession was followed by cries of anguish from the members of the "club," who were distressed by the 75-25 provision, the "partnership" provision, and by the presence in the international oil industry of a tough, capable competitor who did not belong to the club and did not follow its rules. Was the new concession enough of a departure from the old pattern to justify the club's apprehension, and did Mattei's conduct bring chaos to the international oil industry? The answer to both questions is a qualified "no." Time and space are being devoted to these questions and to their answers because one of the chief charges leveled at Mattei, both in Italy and abroad, is that he disrupted a major international industry and ran the risk of losing for Italy many valuable friends.

In the first place, the agreement is not so much of a departure from the pattern as it appears to be, nor is the 75-25 arrangement the greatest departure in the agreement. Because it is the best known, however, it will be considered first. (Note: The figures 75-25 appear nowhere in the agreement.) The agreement calls for a partnership [11] to be established between the National Iranian Oil Company (NIOC) and AGIP Mineraria (the ENI subsidiary that engages in exploration) for the purpose of setting up an operating company of Iranian nationality. Profits from the venture are to be taxed at the rate of 50 per cent by the Iranian government and the balance to be divided equally between the partners (hence the 75-25). AGIP Mineraria must pay all costs of exploration until oil in commercial quantities is discovered and has agreed to spend certain minimum amounts during specified periods of time. These commitments were not great in the case of AGIP: $6,000,000 in four years and a total of $22,000,000 in twelve years. (Pan-American Petroleum Corporation agreed to spend $82,000,000 in the same period of time but has already found deposits several times the size of AGIP's.) However, the costs of exploration are to be recovered by AGIP before the sharing of profits with the Iranian partner commences. This provision now has become rather unattractive to the Iranians in the light of the fact that AGIP has found oil in commercial quantities but not yet "big oil" by Middle Eastern standards. There also has been considerable disgruntlement in Italy at Mattei's agreement to pay 75 per cent, when the others pay only 50 per cent. It should be noted that there was no bonus payment in connection with the ENI concession, although there was a bonus called for in the Pan-American agreement. Unlike most Middle Eastern concession agreements, no responsibilities were imposed on ENI for education, roads, health, or other services, though the same is true of the participants in the Iran Consortium. If moderate quantities of oil are found, the ENI agreement in Iran probably will work out to be very little different from the established pattern of agreement. If lesser quantities are found, it may prove to be better for ENI, but very large quantities of oil over a substantial period of time would give Iran a better deal. All that can be said now is that ENI has still to find "big oil" in Iran.

After the initial reaction the "partnership" idea appears to have been more of a blow to the major oil companies than the 75-25 arrangement. In addition to the partnership itself the board of directors of the operating company is required to be made up one-half of Iranians, with the chairman to be chosen from among the Iranian directors and the vice-chairman and managing director from among the non-Iranians. Certainly the older oil companies in the Middle East were not accustomed to this sort of arrangement and were quite naturally shocked by it. In mitigation of their dire predictions, however, several comments must be made. The "partnership" arrangement probably is superior to what the majors themselves have under the Iran Consortium agreement, where they are not concessionaires at all but simply operating agents of the Iranian government. The Consortium companies operate the facilities without owning any part of them, and most of the oil is purchased at the fields by subsidiaries of the parent companies. Furthermore, it is unlikely that the partnership arrangement will become workable anywhere else in the Middle East for some time to come. Thanks to the British having been in Iran for more than 50 years, to the relatively advanced status of the Iranians, and to the speed with which the Iranians have developed managers and other skilled personnel, Mattei could work out a "partnership" arrangement in Iran. In time, such arrangements will appear elsewhere as well, as they probably would have had there never been a Mattei or an ENI. Furthermore, recent evidence seems to indicate that the Iranians are not entirely satisfied with this provision of the ENI concession. Sharing in the risks and responsibilities is gratifying to national pride and ego, but the certainty involved in the old type of agreement, based on previously determined prices and rates of production costs, and the lack of financial risk, make the new agreement seem much less attractive than it did at the time it was negotiated.

Mattei in Egypt

Mattei's contract with Egypt appears to be even less favorable to ENI than the Iran agreement. Not only is the oil of poor quality and difficult to refine, but also the terms of the contract, so much as is known of them, are extremely unfavorable to Italy. The contract has never been made available for inspection, so some of what is said here must be based on conjecture and speculation rising out of the few facts available. Mattei first entered the Egyptian oil arena in 1955 through a scheme of purchasing shares in oil companies operating in Egypt. More direct activity in Egypt was made possible in 1956 when ENI, through various subsidiaries, acquired 20 per cent of the shares of the International Egyptian Oil Company (IEOC). A Belgian firm, Petrofina, was also a major shareholder. In 1957, Compagnie Orientale des Pétroles (COPE), an operating company, was established by IEOC and the Egyptian government (51 per cent IEOC and 49 per cent by two agencies of the Egyptian government). Through AGIP Mineraria ENI increased its share holdings in IEOC from 1956 to 1960. When the Belgians became unwelcome in Egypt as a result of the Congo crisis in 1960, Petrofina sold its 40 per cent interest in IEOC to ENI at cost, and ENI thus raised its participation to more than 90 per cent. At the same time, share holdings in COPE were adjusted in order that IEOC and the Egyptian government might participate equally.

Mattei agreed to have COPE prospect for oil in Egypt at its own expense and to have the entire production remain at the disposal of the Egyptian government. Egypt takes one-half of the production immediately as a royalty, and apparently can take the other one-half, or so much of it as is desired, for disposition at Egypt's pleasure. Some payment is made to COPE for the portion of COPE's share retained by the Egyptian government but currency regulations probably would prevent the exportation of the payments so made. COPE's production in Egypt has been nearly two million tons a year. In 1959 ENI transported slightly over one million tons of Egyptian crude to Italy but in 1960 only 211,700 tons, although COPE's total production in that year was actually

55,000 tons greater than in 1959. Mattei seems to have tried to cover this questionable bet by selling Nasser $50,000,000 worth of various kinds of petroleum equipment under an arrangement whereby payment was to be made in crude. Thus, even if Egypt elects to keep all of COPE's production under the basic contract, ENI believes that it still can obtain some Egyptian crude through the payment for the equipment. "Waving the banner of revolt against capitalist exploitation," [12] Mattei went into Egypt; he learned a lot during his visit about what exploitation means. It is interesting that Nasser, who led the fight for the Arab League policy against granting concessions to government-owned oil companies, apparently is willing to make an exception in his own country for government-owned ENI.

ENI has concessions in a number of other countries, but most of these arrangements are not very important. The 75-25 arrangement appears here and there. The concession in Libya appears to have some potential in the light of discoveries to date, but the terms of the agreement are more nearly normal in character and not unlike the Libyan concession agreements with other oil companies. Mattei at one time had sought all of the exploration rights in Libya for himself on the rather naive premise that Libya was a former Italian colony, but other oil companies, mostly American, obtained the better concessions.

Mattei's major concession agreements, those with Iran and Egypt, are not particularly favorable to Italy, and the Iran agreement is no longer looked upon with great enthusiasm in Iran. The unusual willingness and speed with which Mattei signed agreements that gave little economic advantage to himself or to Italy lead to the conclusion that Mattei's motives were as often noneconomic as they were economic. In the fact that Mattei's motives were often far outside the scope of his position as head of a public company lay the real dangers of Mattei's operations abroad. A situation where one arm of the Italian state has one foreign policy while the elected government may have another cannot long be tolerated. Had the two policies become more inconsistent, or had the former achieved domination over the latter, the international exploits of Enrico Mattei might have taken on

a completely different and much more ominous appearance. So far
as the oil industry is concerned, some solace may be found in the
hope that if ENI discovers "big oil," its managers may begin to
behave as though ENI were the eighth "sister."

The combination of ENI's statutory mandate as broadly interpreted by Mattei, and the effective organization of ENI and
Mattei's public relations skill, gave Mattei considerable leverage
when it came to negotiating concession agreements with host
countries. He could protect himself at home in Italy, he could
sell himself and his company to the other parties in the agreement,
he could take steps in the direction of doing something about
Italy's energy shortage, and he could accomplish some of his own
personal ends, such as avenging his real or imagined treatment by
the international oil companies and striking a blow for his "antimonopoly" cause.

PUBLIC RELATIONS

"Signor Mattei has acquired an international reputation as a
shrewd, ruthless and rather slippery fighter. But a considerable
part of his success is due to his instinctive understanding of public
relations and to the ability with which he has 'projected an
image.' " [13] Under ordinary circumstances, public relations would
not be considered a measure of performance or a major factor in
economic power, but the quotation from *The Financial Times*
demonstrates why Mattei and ENI are not ordinary circumstances,
and why in this case a review of Mattei's public relations is a
necessary part of this appraisal. The basic question is: How much
of Mattei's power, success, and reputation for success resulted
from his skillful use of practically every known technique of
propaganda? There are two subsidiary questions here also: How
much of Mattei's apparent success was real and not just a matter
of public relations skill, and how much of the real success would
have been achieved without Mattei's "instinctive understanding
of public relations"? Obviously, these questions are not capable
of definitive answers, but considerable insight can be gained by
a judicious examination of the evidence.

Beginnings

There is little doubt now about the genuineness of Mattei's initial success in the Po Valley. He found the gas, he built the pipelines, he got the fields promptly into production, and he provided the industrial North of Italy with large quantities of reasonably priced fuel just at a time when that fuel was most desperately needed. The "Italian miracle" followed. This is the way in which ENI replays postwar history for the Italian public. How much of it is *post hoc ergo propter hoc* reasoning cannot be said with certainty, but the fact remains that a large portion of the vast reserve of public goodwill which ENI enjoys is the result of public belief in the accuracy and relevance of that sequence of events. A public relations slip anywhere along the line could have resulted in a badly mauled Mattei, for he had many enemies in the early days. The high-handed way in which he built the pipelines and the success he had in excluding competition from the Po Valley earned him many more. Had the press or the Communists attacked Mattei at the pipeline stage he might have been brought down, but he never once let the initiative get away from him. Attacks on the "evil monopolies" and reminders of his Partisan activities kept him relatively safe from the far left; his jingoism appealed to the nationalistic right; the northern industrialists were glad to get the fuel; the support, or at least the neutrality, of the press, if it was not already possessed was bought with cash, favors, and friendship (Mattei could be very charming and coöperative when he wanted to be); the politicians were busy with other matters, and besides, Mattei was one of the leaders of the Christian Democratic Party. As a result the public heard only what was good about Mattei and the Po gas. At the very least the success in the Po Valley was protected by careful and effective public relations.

The successes of those early days only reinforced Mattei's preoccupation with public relations, and he began very early to collect and analyze adverse press comment. After ENI came into existence, these collections were published annually in a series of volumes entitled *Stampa e Oro Nero* (The Press and Black

Gold). It is perhaps significant that the size of the annual collection has been steadily decreasing in recent years.[14] Mattei had a way with the press. He was almost always accessible by telephone, day or night, and often called individual reporters with scoops or stories. It paid in many ways for a newspaperman to be on friendly terms with Mattei. Persistent criticism of Mattei was lacking, except in a handful of extremist magazines, both left and right. The daily press was largely friendly or neutral, including most of the business and financial press, which was for a long time hostile. Most of the criticism of Mattei, even by the responsible press, was documented largely with rumors and was poorly framed; this probably was a tribute to the success with which Mattei was able to keep secret the really important data on his company. Many of the attacks were strident in tone, were met by vitriolic replies, and soon deteriorated into irrelevancies. A recent series of articles by Indro Montanelli in *Corriere della Sera* avoided many of these shortcomings, but, through no great fault of his, the writer was still forced to rely heavily on rumor, hearsay, inference, and innuendo, and as a result the articles were full of incorrect information. Mattei treated almost any attack on him or on his company as being of sufficient importance to justify his personal reply. His rely to Montanelli, and Montanelli's rebuttal, occupied more than a full page of *Corriere* only a month before Mattei's death and was proclaimed in headlines of "a size and character reserved for declarations of war." [15] It is interesting to observe that the treatment of Mattei by the small portion of the press hostile to him was usually much more fair than was *Il Giorno's* treatment of Mattei's critics.

ENI's own initiative in public relations work, combined with a friendly or neutral press, made it possible for Mattei to take risks that otherwise might have been too great. His oil deal with the Russians, for example, was not popular in Italy, but the press did not play up the opposition for what it was worth, and Mattei was busy selling the arrangement as a way to bring cheaper gasoline to the Italian motorist. He branded the opposition as tools of the international petroleum monopoly and claimed that group had forced him into a position where he had to buy Russian oil.

The storm over that deal apparently has passed. Whether ENI could get away with a major extension of the contract with the USSR now is a moot question. Mattei stuck his neck out by emphasizing the short four-year term of the Russian contract and the decreasing percentage of purchases from that source, but the chances for other public relations successes in this area without Mattei probably are pretty good. Strangely enough, at the time there was almost no comment in Italy on the fact that Mattei apparently had concluded the Russian oil deal before he mentioned the negotiations to the government.

Il Giorno

Il Giorno, ENI's newspaper, plays an important role in ENI's public relations activities and, except when Mattei or his companies are an issue, is an excellent Italian journal. In layout, coverage, and features it is patterned after the best English and American newspapers. That it is as good as it is comes as somewhat of a surprise. The first editor remained for only a short time, then left *Il Giorno* and edited a far-left news magazine through which he served as Mattei's most consistent and vitriolic critic. Another editor of *Il Giorno* was not a professional journalist but a politician who previously had been vice-secretary general of the Italian Socialist Party. When responding to attacks on Mattei or ENI, or when promoting some of Mattei's controversial policies, *Il Giorno* became a rival of the Communist press in stridency and vitriol. Objectivity disappeared, and misstatements, false statements, character assassination, and incredible irrelevancy took over—not only in the editorial comment but also in the purported news stories. The Italian press is inclined towards being a bit volatile anyway, but *Il Giorno*, during the Gulf-Ragusa controversy in the fall of 1961, gave the other newspapers a few pointers.[16] In terms of newspaper policy all of this is interesting; in terms of a state-owned oil company's publishing such a journal it is nothing less than fantastic.

Mattei's Interpersonal Relations

Mattei's own public appearances, which he hated and resisted, usually were not very impressive. He was not a good public speaker, and often his unpolished manner and lack of broad knowledge showed through even the best prepared speeches. In a 1961 television interview Mattei was wandering, evasive, inaccurate, vindictive, very political, and highly nationalistic. He was not at his best in groups or where he faced open opposition. He was most effective in planning strategy, working behind the scenes, or in dealing face to face with one or two individuals. In public his tone often became sharp and his manner vindictive and harsh. Mattei carried these same limitations into his interpersonal relations within the ENI Group. Most of Mattei's contacts with his own people were on an individual basis. Although many committees and boards appear in the ENI table of organization, they rarely met and then only for formal or procedural purposes, not for purposes of consultation or discussion. I was surprised to find that, generally speaking, the officers, including senior ones, in the various companies of the ENI Group did not know each other very well. Top-level line officers of AGIP, for example, did not know their counterparts in SNAM or ANIC. Upon inquiry I learned that Mattei never assembled company people in groups and that they were not encouraged to get together, especially across company lines. On very rare occasions, usually not more than once or twice a year, senior people were brought together under very formal circumstances, such as for the purpose of meeting Russian Vice-Premier Kosygin when he visited the Milan offices of ENI in 1961.[17]

Technique

Mattei was extremely fond of pointing out the shortcomings of private industry, especially large private industry, and accompanied such statements with contrasting illustrations of ENI's exemplary performance. Attention often was drawn to the relatively small subsidy with which ENI made its debut and the great size to which the company grew under Mattei's tutelage without any further subsidies from the government. In these pronouncements no mention was made of the gross undervaluation of the assets involved in the subsidy; of ENI's virtually tax-free status; of the fact that ENI does not, except in Sicily,[18] pay to the state the oil and gas royalties that a private company would; of the extent to which the Po Valley gas profits provide the means for ENI's growth; or of how much of the expansion has been financed by bond issues and other borrowing leniently authorized and guaranteed by the government. There is no doubt that Mattei's public relations accentuated the positive, as any public relations effort probably should, but the question with ENI is whether the public relations of a government corporation should use this technique so strenuously that it becomes an overt attack on the private sector of the economy and sometimes on the government itself. Unfortunately, few Italians have yet been inclined to examine ENI and Mattei except through rose-colored glasses of Mattei manufacture.

So important, so complete, and so all-encompassing was Mattei's concept of public relations that the public relations function is one of ENI's major activities, permeates most aspects of the operation, and was personally supervised by Mattei. The subsections of the public relations division present an interesting picture: "press office," "speeches and publications," "advertising," "protocol office," "social studies," "economic studies," and "government relations." In the intervention-free paradise which ENI occupied, the "government relations" section of this government corporation was primarily concerned with watching proposed legislation for possible (and usually inadvertent) effects on ENI and its operations. That a government-owned company should have in its public relations division a section called "government relations" is a good indication of the independent status in which Mattei saw his company.

Mattei seemed to see all advertising as a public relations as well as a political function and he insisted that advertising, in all its phases, be handled centrally and not by the operating companies. The social and economic studies groups are essentially research and advisory offices designed primarily to assess social and economic effects and reactions to price and product changes, plant locations and other moves, both consummated and contemplated. Mattei, however, often took important actions without ever consulting either group.

One important change which Mattei's public relations consciousness worked in Italy was to provide the country with a system of service stations concerned as much with service as with peddling petroleum products. Until the Mattei era, the Italian service station consisted of a gas pump and a canvas chair for the attendant. In most of them, the customer's automobile stood in the public street while being refueled, and the only restrooms were the open fields or public *pissoirs* that might chance to be in the neighborhood (available to everyone, except persons of the female sex). The AGIP stations have changed all this, and many of them would compete effectively in attractiveness and convenience with the best service stations in the United States. Clean restrooms, showers, bars and restaurants, ample parking space, and motel facilities accompany the standard accoutrements of a well-equipped service station. Service pays; AGIP now is approaching one-third of the Italian gasoline business; the six-legged-dog is at your service everywhere. Competitors are forced to provide more service too, but most of them without the verve and imagination of AGIP. Not all of Mattei's public relations, then, were concerned with high-level economic or political policy.

The scope of his reach in this field is awe inspiring. On April 30, 1961, ENI submitted to the government its "Annual Report and Statement of Accounts" and an accompanying survey of "Energy and Hydrocarbons." The two documents together added up to 351 pages of beautifully bound and illustrated public relations material and four pages of accounts. From these documents it was possible to learn the location, type, and capacity of every nuclear power station in the world, whether planned, under construction or in operation; the consumption per hectare of nitrogenous fertilizer in almost every country in the world and the average annual percentage change between 1953–54 and 1958–59; the production of natural and synthetic rubber by country for 1950, 1959, and 1960; the chief oil and gas discoveries throughout the world by area, company, and type; and the number of crew months spent in 1960 by AGIP Mineraria and its contractors on gravimetric and seismic geophysical surveys; but it cannot be determined, from these documents or from any other source, how much methane remains in the Po deposits, how much capital ENI is expending abroad in exploration, how much oil ENI produced abroad for the Italian market, the volume of ENI's sales in foreign countries, or what is really planned for the vast petrochemical and thermoelectrical complex being constructed at Gela.

One also discovers that "ENI's activities . . . are the result of a combination of directives and decisions which are taken within the framework of a coherent scheme for promoting the national interest" and that "this scheme was clearly explained by the Minister of State Participations in a Program Report submitted to Parliament early in 1961," [19] leaving the impression that ENI operates under the directives of the Minister of State Participations. The Program Report referred to undoubtedly was dictated, in large part, by Mattei himself; no specific directive from the Minister is mentioned or referred to in any way; and, anyhow, the present Minister is Mattei's former legal counsel. These ENI documents are full of diatribes against private business, against the international petroleum "monopolies," and in praise of ENI's battle with these sources of evil. The annual reports, and often accompanying surveys, are public-relations-oriented from the luxurious binding and the full-color photographic reproductions and lavish charts to the tone of the contents. These reports are not addressed to a supervising minister but to the politicians, the press, and the public and, consistent with Mattei's very broad view of public relations, are published in several languages. There was something for everybody in Mattei's public relations.

During the attempt of the Communist Deputies in the Sicilian Regional Assembly to revoke the Gulf concession at Ragusa, Mattei took different stands for different people and said different things in different places. While Mattei was denying that he wanted the Ragusa concession for himself, Il Giorno was vehemently supporting the Communist move, strenuously attacking Gulf, and the "foreign oil monopolists," and encouraging the substitution of a public company. One day *Il Giorno* attacked Gulf because it paid only 12.5 per cent royalty to the Sicilian government; the next day the paper defended ENI's own 4 per cent royalty in Sicily by pointing out how poor was the quality of the Gela deposits; another day *Il Giorno* boasted about the billions of lire that ENI was investing in its great refineries and petrochemical installations at Gela and reminded Italy of the wonderful job that had been done in the Po Valley, where ENI pays no royalties at all.

The Communist newspaper *L'Unità*, on November 9, 1958, charged that the American armed forces had seized the geological studies of the Sicilian subsurface from the files of the Ministry of Agriculture and had turned them over to the Gulf Oil Corporation, which then was easily able to find large deposits of oil in the Ragusa field. The Gulf Company promptly sued *L'Unità* and the author of the charges for libel and obtained a retraction on July 22, 1960. On October 15, 1961, at the beginning of the Ragusa controversy, *Il Giorno* again accused Gulf of having used these same seized AGIP archives in order to find oil in Sicily. When Gulf's Italian representative called the attention of *Il Giorno* to the earlier charges, the libel action and the retraction, *Il Giorno* replied by accusing Gulf of hiring incompetent technicians who did not have the sense to use the AGIP surveys which were then in existence. *Il Giorno* during this phase of the controversy failed to mention an AGIP report of December 18, 1945, which stated: "From the foregoing we may conclude that hydrocarbon exploration in Sicily is extremely difficult and fraught with uncertainties, and that consequently AGIP should be advised to abandon these areas completely." [20] At no time during the Ragusa dispute in 1961 did *Il Giorno* print or quote any major part of Gulf's replies to *Il Giorno*'s violent charges.

Mattei was very fond of accusing the foreign oil "monopolists" of fantastic profit margins; forty-five [21] and seventy-five [22] per cent profits were his favorite statistics. These figures are tossed about with great abandon, without substantiating evidence. Nor is there ever an explanation for the inability of ENI to reduce its own prices any further if the profit margins in the industry are so large. The double talk and unsubstantiated charges were standard behavior in Mattei's public relations. The vague and unresponsive reply was another Mattei technique. When a commission appointed in 1956 by the Ministry of Industry and Commerce to ration the supply of methane from the Po Valley asked Mattei how large the Po deposits were, he replied: ". . . publication of data relating to gas reserves . . . cannot be considered without infringing on the legal position and practice of the distributing company." [23] When charged with monopolistic behavior, Mattei replied: "The legend that ENI is a monopoly has been built on its exclusive rights to prospect for hydrocarbons in the Po Valley —that is to say in a sixth of the country's territory. No mention is made of the fact that in the rest of Italy, where prospecting is open to all, four out of five of the important finds have been made by ENI competing against other companies. Nor is it mentioned that the big oil companies have dozens of concessions throughout the world, each of which is many times larger than the Po Valley." [24] When charged with concealing the disposition of the profits from the Po gas, Mattei replied: "To calculate the net profits of the ENI Group one need only examine the consolidated balance sheet on page 25" [of the ENI Report].[25] From that balance sheet, one could learn almost nothing about any phase of ENI, much less about the disposition of the Po profits.

The basic themes running through all of Mattei's public relations efforts were those of the little, humble, faithful Italian public servant following the directives of his government in carrying on the titantic struggle against the evil, unscrupulous, profit-grabbing foreign monopolists who had conspired to keep Italy from obtaining what was rightfully hers. The little, loyal public servant not only obeyed his government's orders but implored its written approval before taking any action. He was constantly besieged by requests from government officials and ministries for the minutest details of his operations, but he supplied these details promptly, willingly, and without complaint. He was embarrassed and humiliated, for Italy, when the powerful foreign capitalist profit-mongers failed to offer Italy an interest in the Iran Consortium. But he was also a raging lion who, on behalf of Italy, taught her oppressors a lesson and made them feel the full weight of Italy's righteous wrath. Because success is the reward of the just, every battle was fought through to a triumphant conclusion against overwhelming, almost insurmountable, odds.

Taken all together, Mattei's public relations were intelligent, imaginative, well-timed, and successful, though often of doubtful probity and taste. He created the personal and corporate images he desired; he won immense public support through much better service, slightly lower prices, and carefully thought out explanations thereof; he had a large portion of the press on his side; he turned even some very doubtful activities into public triumphs. It can be said with considerable conviction that much of Mattei's power and success were brought about or enhanced by his public relations policies, and, with equal conviction, that a large part of his reputation for success was not based on real success at all but was the result of carefully planned and carried out public relations activities. How long the undeserved portion of Mattei's reputation for success can continue to live is not an easy question to answer. More real success by ENI may solve the problem, such as finding "big oil" in the Middle East. Without this or comparable achievements to replace the Po Valley natural gas, ENI may soon be faced with lessened support from press and public and increased interrogation and intervention from the government, and a fall of ENI from its position of high favor probably will be one of the inevitable consequences of Mattei's death.

It is doubtful if Mattei could have built, maintained, or utilized his great political, social, and economic power without the benefit of his public relations skill and public relations triumphs. He realized from the beginning, as others are just coming to realize, the enormous power and leverage which successful public relations efforts could provide for him and for his company. As is pointed out in greater detail in the next chapter, much of political, social, and economic power depends upon favorable public opinion for its existence. Mattei seemed instinctively to see that effective public relations could produce power, create the illusion of power (in itself a form of power), and protect existing power from attack. We proceed now to a more detailed discussion of this and other facets of the phenomena of power.

CHAPTER 5

A Case Study
in Power

"Power," like "morality," "right," and other fighting abstractions, has always been largely at the mercy of highly subjective and emotional analysis.[1] The ease with which the concept of power at first glance promises to reduce itself to manageable form is soon dispelled as one begins to look for firm foundations on which to rest his investigation. Just as with attempts to conceptualize "good" and "evil" (and these ideas have been closely intermingled with the idea of "power"), the harder the effort the deeper is the realization that the terms cannot be used objectively unless the sense in which and the intent with which each is employed are accurately made known. Consequently, a few pages are here devoted to establishing a common concept of power on the basis of which our study may continue.

Having painted the background against which the drama of power was played in a concentrated decade of maneuver and manipulation by ENI and its fabulous Mattei, we come now to consider the power relationships that were the keys to Mattei's success and to ENI's growth, and the wonder of modern Europe. An observer, in order to assess the power elements involved in a study such as this, must have in hand all available facts, historic sequences, and have clarified the environment in which they took place. Dealing in an abstract conception may then come more easily.

The problem is not essentially one of defining the term "power."

Although differences of scope and detail exist, there is remarkably little variation in definitions of "power," even as between sociologists on one hand and political scientists on the other, or as between ancients and moderns. The trouble lies in the concepts behind the definitions and in the lack of common understanding of the power relationship. That power was a relationship at all was realized rather late, and the recognition of the truly reciprocal nature of the relationship has occurred only in this century.

A MODERN CONCEPT OF POWER

Modern concepts of power include within their boundaries substantial recognition of other important factors which influence social events. In concept at least, power has become a sort of reservoir of related factors that are significant in the determination of social affairs. So long as the concept being employed is one of this type, the risk of missing the crucial interplay of other factors is considerably reduced.

The traditional concepts of power and its limitations now seem a bit plaintive and naive. The traditional limitations on power "have faded like lost saints, cherished but invoked in vain. The old way of stating the problem—power *and* society, politics *and* law, *and* custom, *and* morals—is unreal, for power is reluctant, if not absolutely unwilling, to enter into partnerships." [2]

Power is the capacity or ability of an individual, or a group of individuals, to determine the behavior [3] ("influence behavior," [4] "exercise ascendancy over," [5] "modify conduct," [6] or "control" [7]) other individuals or groups in accordance with his own wishes. Almost no one would quarrel with the basic characteristics of this definition. In keeping with the current tendency to qualify all statements with the language of statistics or of probability theory, however, Gerth and Mills have modified it by adding that power "is simply the probability that men will act as another man wishes." [8] Talcott Parsons broadens the scope of power to the "capacity to mobilize the resources of the society for the attainment of goals," and thus calls attention to the operation of power outside the realm of individuals and groups. He goes on to say, however, that power "is mobilization, above all, of the action of persons and groups." [9]

Whether the exercise of power must rest on real or threatened violence or naked force has long been a point of contention among power philosophers. The consensus today probably is that it does not need to rest on violence. As neatly expressed by Lasswell, "(p)ower may rest on faiths and loyalties as well as interests, to say nothing of habit and apathy. And even when the element of constraint is prominent, it need not take the form of violence. Sanctions may be applied with regard to values other than physical safety and well-being." [10] Power operates with the help of actual or threatened severe deprivations for nonconformity, but need not involve violence. It is a "paradox of power" [11] that it is most secure when it is not under the necessity of showing itself in the form of naked force; when naked force must be used, power is, necessarily, under attack.

"Modern" concepts of power are characterized, I think, by three primary assumptions: (1) that power is a resource of society which can be used to solve some of society's problems; [12] that power is itself a source of order; [13] though subject to abuse and corruption, power has a positive as well as a negative side; (2) that power is essentially a relationship between individual and individual, between individual and group, between group and group; that the relationship is reciprocal in nature, requiring "empowering responses" for its existence; [14] that power is based, in large measure, "on interpersonal expectations and attitudes;" [15] (3) that power, like wealth, is not static in quantity but is constantly being produced. Traditional concepts of power were almost invariably concerned with power in a strictly political setting, but modern concepts cover the whole range of social experience. Political theorists were primarily responsible for the first of the primary elements, sociologists [16] for the second, and the members of a number of different disciplines, including economics, for the third.

A workable concept of power can be stated as follows: Power is a reciprocal relationship both within and among all political, social, economic, and other types of power systems; it is dynamic and changing with regard to quantity and to form; it is one of the vital resources of society but, like wealth and some other resources, is subject to abuse and corruption.

To this basic concept should be appended several additional considerations. Beliefs are important to the production, maintenance, and exercise of power; ideas affect institutions as well as conduct. The traditional mental picture of the term "power," a picture of the many ruled by one power holder, does not exist in fact; power is always hierarchical.[17] "Forms of power and influence are agglutinative: those with some forms tend to acquire other forms also." [18] None of the forms of power, generally speaking, can stand alone, as each requires the simultaneous exercise of other forms as well; and none of the forms is basic to all the others.[19]

A few general comments in regard to the sources of power are in order. Power may come from personality, strategic geographical location, wealth, control of one or more factors of production, fear, position, superior intelligence, superior physical strength, age, ideas, beliefs, and from a thousand other sources, but does this approach give us an accurate picture and a useful tool of analysis? Roberto Michels argues that power, even that which is of personal origin, is created and maintained by public opinion, which in turn is "conditioned by sentiment, affection, reverence, or fatalism." [20] The "public" whose opinion counts for so much in this analysis may be very large or very small depending upon the type of power and the circumstances surrounding it. This view is consistent with modern concepts of power and especially with sociological concepts. It recognizes the reciprocal nature of the power relationship and the need for an obedient subject as well as for a holder of power.

It is accurate to say that both men and organizations are capable of holding power, and it is obvious that men may wield power. But can it be said that an organization wields or exercises power? Considerable confusion exists around the answer to this question. On one level, it does no particular harm to say that General Motors or ENI exercises power. It is both a semantic convenience (because it is easier than trying to locate and describe or name the individuals who participate in the activities of General Motors) and a statement containing an element of truth. So long as one realizes that men make the decisions which direct the wielding of power, it probably is no more inaccurate to say that General Motors wields power than it is to say that the SS *United States* carries passengers. As we have seen before, power is hierarchical. It is the hierarchy or organization, consisting of men, that wields power. One man, even in the most absolute of dictatorships, does not, by himself, wield power; without the consent and coöperation of the men in his hierarchy, he wields only as much power as his physical attributes can induce. On another level, of course, it "cannot be emphasized enough that institutions as such never exercise power; it is always the men in charge of the institutions." [21]

In the case of ENI, however, the problem is simplified. Often, there is no identifiable individual or group of individuals who can be said to wield power in an organization, and one is forced, for want of any other way of doing it, to describe the power wielder as General Motors or Great Britain. But to a greater extent than is usually true, whether one says "ENI" or "Enrico Mattei," the meaning is essentially the same. ENI was simply the instrumentality through which Mattei, on the highest level, wielded power, through a hierarchy, of course.

Although our study is concerned with power phenomena in and around a particular public corporation and its late president, it must still be recognized that what will have to be considered is not just one power center but several overlapping ones. Mattei was one power center, ENI another, and the combination yet a third; each of the companies in the ENI Group is a power center, as is each of the many possible combinations thereof; Mattei was one power center with regard to Italy's domestic economy, another in Italy's domestic politics, and still another in Italy's foreign policy. Obviously, it will not be feasible to establish clearly in every case which center of power is at issue and, actually, little effort will be made to do this at all, but it should be noted that what appears on the surface to be a relatively simple power center proves to be a very complex one with many of the same character-

istics as the incredibly involved network of power relationships
and centers in society as a whole. Our investigation is limited to
the power centers at the highest levels of the ENI Group, and
of the Italian government, and will delve not at all into the
numerous power centers located all up and down and through
the complicated organization; but the latter, if examined, would
differ very little from interpersonal and interpositional relationships in any large modern business organization. Even the relatively small number of power relationships we have retained
within our scope provides a host of complicating factors.

Some of the power centers in and around ENI, as one might
expect, are personal in character, some economic, some political,
some strategic, and some legal, and the limits upon the exercise
of the power are of the same heterogeneous variety. The social
order is a limitation on power, as are technical factors of transportation and communication and the physical and psychological
characteristics of the individuals. The mores of the Italian people
and certain national characteristics serve both to create and maintain and to limit power. It will be seen that legal limitations are
not extensive, either in theory or in practice. Whether this is because, as Hillenbrand puts it, modern legal theory "woefully
fails to come to grips with the essential problem of power, the
prevention of the use of which is a primary function of law," [22] or
because the available theory has simply not been employed is a
subject of considerable controversy.

A major issue raised elsewhere in this study is whether ENI,
as a public corporation, should be considered as a manifestation
of governmental power, or whether, as a virtually autonomous
economic entity, it should be looked upon as nongovernmental.
Reactions both in Italy and abroad to Mattei's exercises of power
would tend to the conclusion that public opinion often looks
upon ENI as nongovernmental. The Arab League, for example,
with a strong and clear-cut policy against participation by foreign governments in oil concessions in Arab countries, has been
most hospitable to ENI. Furthermore, it would take careful reading of the Italian press, especially the small portion of it that
occasionally attacked Mattei, to discover that ENI is indeed a

wholly government-owned corporation. If in truth it should be considered a nongovernmental power center, several possible conclusions may be drawn. Chief among these is the possibility that under certain circumstances the government is unable to control oppressive acts even when they run counter to the law.

"The history of vigilante movements in America, of lynchings and race riots, of the many and varied forms of discrimination that reflect deep-seated prejudices, and the like, suggests that even where the government may seek to enforce the law—which in the instances cited it does not always do—the climate of opinion may be such as to foredoom that effort. In some cases, indeed, the temper of public opinion or of public sentiment may actually sustain, where it does not initially compel, the abusive acts of governments themselves. . . . Democratic governments do not move in a vacuum. They respond, as they should respond, to the changing tides of public opinion. Consequently, to subject the ruler to the will of the electorate is no sure protection against oppression unless that electorate is itself determined not to tolerate abusive rule." [23]

Thus, for our purposes it probably makes little difference whether we consider ENI to be a governmental or a nongovernmental organization.

Formal limits on ENI's and Mattei's power were relatively few, but this does not mean, necessarily, that ENI and Mattei could act without restraint. Public opinion in Italy is capable of switching very rapidly; some of the sources of power are sufficiently volatile in nature that they may change overnight from a source of power into a competing power center; outside Italy, the principal power of ENI and of Mattei was to disrupt existing economic and political patterns, and in this arena there are many competitive power centers of both governmental and nongovernmental character. Mattei's preoccupation with matters of public relations is evidence that he was well aware of at least one of the boundaries, albeit a shifting one, of his and ENI's power. In the remainder of this chapter, we shall examine these and many other related aspects of ENI power phenomena. It is obvious that

Mattei's death has already altered substantially most aspects of the power here under discussion.

A MODERN PHENOMENON OF POWER

From the first significant demonstration of his power, the day he refused to obey his government's order to liquidate the assets of AGIP and succeeded in his rebellion, through the high-handed building of the pipelines and the exclusion of competition from the Po Valley, to the negotiation of the Iran concession, the 1957 Oil Law, the Soviet oil contract, and the day of his death, more and more of the value positions of the Italian government, in both the domestic and the foreign spheres, were made or profoundly influenced by Enrico Mattei. From the refusal to obey the liquidation order, through the era of the ineffectual supervisory committee of ministers, to the day a former associate became Minister of State Participations, it was increasingly clear that Mattei operated largely without government restraint. The "grey eminence" of the Italian government was not a myth but a fact. The first three chapters of this study have traced the development of this power phenomenon and have examined its scope and manifestations. In the first part of this chapter we have developed a modern concept of power; the following section will be devoted to a review of the phenomenon of power within the conceptual framework.

The first step will be to consider the environment of Mattei's power, the circumstances and characteristics that control the scope of the power, and the manner of its exercise. One of the chief contrasts between modern concepts of power and traditional ones is the shift of emphasis from the "by whom" and "over whom" variety of power question to the "under what circumstances." After scrutinizing the environment of the power, we shall briefly reëxamine the sources or foundations of Mattei's power. In one important sense, these two subjects are really the same; the characteristics of the environment are often also sources of power, and a national characteristic or tradition may be the very foundation upon which a system of power is built. For the purposes of this discussion, however, making a distinction is justified by the obvious expositional advantages of being able to examine the roots of the power apart from the soil in which they thrive. Also closely related to, and even intermingled with, the environment and the foundations are the limits and boundaries of the power, but again the subject matter will be considered separately in order to achieve expositional ends.

In the last section of this chapter we shall make a direct application of power theory to power as practiced by Mattei and ENI, and the basic elements of our power concept will be tested against actual power situations.

It is wise to be reminded at this time that Mattei and ENI cannot safely be distinguished from each other in our discussion. The latter, for the purposes of power analysis, is the alter ego of the former. To say that ENI was the *only* instrument of Mattei's power, and for this reason not required to be distinguished, would be somewhat misleading; much of Mattei's power was exercised outside the framework of the company which he headed. Because of its size and organization and because of its position in the Italian economy, ENI possessed considerable power of its own (though largely economic) apart from Mattei. ENI's own power, however, was not very different from what one would expect to find in any large business organization and did not result in unusual manifestations.

Environment of Mattei's Power

Denis Mack Smith, in his excellent new modern history of Italy, wrote: "From Rienzi to Masaniello and D'Annunzio there had been many notable demagogues before Mussolini, and Gregorovius in the nineteenth century said that he found three types constantly recurring in Italian history—Machiavelli, Cesare Borgia, and the condottieri." [24] In a *Reporter* article in 1958, Claire Sterling called Mattei "Italy's modern condottiere." [25] Sterling oversimplified. Mattei was more nearly a combination of all three, with a large portion of John D. Rockefeller thrown in. Both Sterling and Mack Smith remind us, however, that neither Mattei nor any other modern Italian institution or public figure can be ap-

praised outside the cultural environment and background and the
Italian national character. Of course, this is true to some extent of
any country, but in Italy it is true to a greater extent than in
most, and, fortunately, the trail in Italy is a relatively easy one
to follow.

Obviously, not all traits of a national character or facets of the
cultural environment are relevant to our subject, and not all of
the relevant traits or facets are of sufficient importance to justify
treatment here. Actually, only three aspects of ENI's and Mattei's
environment will be examined. Two traits of national character
are of particular importance in any attempt to understand the
ENI situation: an ineradicable strain of anarchism and a widespread jingoism. The Italian antimonopoly tradition and its im-
plementing public policies will be given brief attention. The last
environmental factor to be considered will be the power vacuum
created by the weak government.

National character. The most important trait to be pondered is
the instinctive Italian habit of disobedience and disrespect for
law. It has been said that the amazing individualism of the Italians
is both their greatest glory and their direst peril. Anyone who
has ever driven an automobile in Italy would agree wholeheartedly
with the latter characterization. These habits are very old but assumed a national character after the *Risorgimento.* Politicians
fought duels among themselves at the same time as they were
trying to punish crimes of violence. Garibaldi raised a succession
of private armies. Further evidence is seen in the frequent student
riots against university discipline and in the complete lack of willingness to queue up and take one's turn, whether at the stamp
window at a post office, the door to a public conveyance, or a
theater exit. Italian traffic and driving habits are a national dis-
grace, paid for by one of the highest automobile death and ac-
cident rates in the world. An Italian with his first automobile
and six weeks' driving experience sees himself as the drag cham-
pion of the *autostrada.* Speed limits, stop signs, and "no passing"
zones vanish in a heady miasma of individualism and virility. The
anarchism of Italian traffic is perhaps the modern epitome of this
facet of the national character.

In order to avoid blanket condemnation of Mattei on Anglo-Saxon terms for his failure to carry out instructions, for his high-handed and illegal methods used in building the first pipelines, for his habit of acting first and consulting the government later, and for his many other illegal and extralegal activities and behavior, it must be recognized that most Italians do not condemn him for this. The national habit of anarchism runs strong and deep. A generation of Fascism and years of German occupation only strengthened the tendency. The Italian motorist who obeys the traffic laws is so rare as to be almost without example. The motorists' behavior toward fire trucks, police cars, and other emergency vehicles would lead to wholesale fines and imprisonment in almost any other country in the world, but in Italy it goes unnoticed, except by the wide-eyed visitor. In spite of specific prohibitory laws in most cities, New Year's Eve in Italy is still the occasion for throwing one's empty bottles, broken furniture, tin cans, and garbage into the streets, at no little risk to the life and limb of the passersby; side streets often are blocked to traffic for several days. Much of what Mattei has done differs only in degree or locale from what the ordinary Italian does as a part of his daily life.

Disobedience is prevalent in the economic sectors too—prevalent, expected, and accepted. The payment of income tax still is a game and not a duty. Many of the rich still pay no income taxes at all, and gross understatements of income are expected of those who do file returns. The individual income tax form, comparable to Form 1040 in the United States, has separate columns for the taxpayer's figures, for the tax collector's estimates and for their compromise.

A casual attitude toward statutory mandates, prohibitions and procedures is commonplace. Even the Constitution is subjected to the same kind of treatment. Article 100 of the Constitution of 1948 provided for a Court of Accounts (Corte dei Conti) to audit the government's budget and to control the financial administration of all public agencies and corporations, but Article 100 was not implemented for many years after the Constitution went into effect and still has not received enough legislative attention to make it in any real sense viable. A "delegate" of the Court of Accounts is required by law [26] to sit with ENI's board of directors and board of auditors in order to exercise the control described in Article 100 of the Constitution, but this functionary is no less a formality or rubber stamp than the other control institutions in the ENI structure. Italian law is full of checks, controls, audits, reports, and other procedures designed to facilitate supervision by the government of its many agencies and corporations, but most of them are ignored or recognized only in terms of meaningless formalities. Mattei's failure, in some cases, even to go through the motions and his general disregard for the substance of the control procedures have their counterparts in all walks of Italian public and private life. Even Mussolini complained that he was the most disobeyed man in Italian history.

On the theory that the failure of public agencies to comply with audit and control procedures was due, in part, to the bewildering, confusing, and contradictory array of such procedures and to the lack of centralized responsibility in any one ministry or bureau, a new ministry (Ministry of State Participations) was created in 1956,[27] and to it was assigned the bulk of the responsibility for supervising government corporations and agencies in the economic sector. Early drafts of the law setting up the new ministry had been influenced by members of Parliament who saw the ministry as a way of bringing ENI and Mattei under government control, but the final draft of the statute did little more than substitute the new ministry for the Ministry of Finance in the already existing supervisory functions. Almost everything else was left unchanged. Some additional report procedures were provided for, but no machinery for auditing the information provided by ENI and the other public companies. The government has no more control over ENI through the new Ministry than it had under the old arrangements. Even if the statute creating the Ministry of State Participations had teeth, which it does not, it probably would not have affected Mattei or ENI. Nobody could have been appointed to the Ministry without Mattei's approval.

In an environment where lawlessness is a trait of the national character, Mattei's conduct does not attract the attention it would attract under other circumstances. In terms of relative values, were lawlessness and disregard for legal procedures less accepted and more condemned, they might tend to outweigh, or at least considerably mitigate, the beneficial and positive results to which Mattei was always able to point. In view of recent public attitudes in Italy, however, the scope of Mattei's power was markedly extended by the lack of genuine concern over the ways in which he achieved many of his ends. This lack of concern among Italians ranges far beyond Mattei's activities within the borders of Italy and seems to include his important role in determining Italy's positions in foreign policy and his disregard for principles and routines whose origins are not Italian but are international or multinational in character. This favorable, or rather not unfavorable, public opinion which Mattei enjoyed in Italy protected, supported, and enhanced the power he wielded. The importance to power of the climate of public opinion is clearly illustrated.

The role that habits of lawlessness played in Mattei's exercise of power were largely inadvertent on his part, though sometimes he may consciously have decided to go a little farther than he would have if it had not been for the protection he thus enjoyed. I do not believe that Mattei often intentionally took advantage of the Italian propensity for anarchism. On the other hand, I think that Mattei did take intentional advantage of the Italian antiforeign and jingoistic bent. He obviously possessed the bent himself, but nevertheless was objective enough to recognize the value to him of its presence among Italians generally. He pursued and encouraged the theme from the very first days of his association with the defunct AGIP. It always played an important role in his public relations activities, and he used it with considerable skill.

In any country, jingoism usually develops out of perfectly natural and healthy roots, as patriotism or justifiable pride of accomplishment. The *Risorgimento* in Italy gave increased strength and unity to Italian patriotism, but these healthy feelings were soon carried to excess. From Mazzini's characterization of the

Italians as the "Messiah people," through protests against foreign words becoming a part of the language, to Mussolini's "mare nostrum," the jingoism has evolved. World War II removed it from the expressed part of Italian policy, but Mattei helped to promote its return. At a time when official pronouncements of Italian policy were all of international coöperation, free competition, and the brotherhood of man, Mattei was promoting his monopoly in the Po Valley with strident cries of "foreign monopolies," "rapacious foreigners," "sacred Italian treasure chest," and "the enemy from abroad." When official Italy was trying to live down Mussolini's "mare nostrum," Mattei was claiming the Mediterranean, Africa, and even the Middle East as "natural spheres of Italian influence." While the Italian government was clearing away the wreckage caused by Mussolini's paranoid ambitions, Mattei was demanding that Italy be allowed to "assume her rightful place among the nations of the world." While Italy was accepting massive foreign economic aid, Mattei was busy making "Italy a country to reckon with on all the markets of the world." [28] Mattei's cries reached sympathetic ears, even in the government.

Again a trait of national character enhanced Mattei's power and gave him space in which to exercise it. Failures could be turned into triumphs, losses into gains, high prices into low prices, and the Russian oil deal into an Italian victory simply by injecting into the situation a reasonable appeal to national vanity or to an antiforeign inclination. The Russian oil contract could have brought an end to Mattei's power, for several reasons, had he not been able to sweeten the pill with a blow at the international oil companies (and a small reduction in the price of gasoline). The pride of Italians at having an aggressive oil company of their own, resulting in large part from Mattei's public relations activities, made it possible for Mattei to escape censure for acts which might otherwise have been his ruin.

Antimonopoly tradition. In spite of not being old enough or deeply enough ingrained to be a trait of the national character, Italy's antimonopoly tradition is nonetheless an important factor in ENI's power environment. An integral part of the tradition is the assumption that direct government intervention in the economic sector is the only feasible way of dealing with private monopoly power. Italy has been plagued by highhanded industrial monopolies during most of its modern history, and a strong tradition of opposition to such centers of monopoly has developed. Yet legislative attempts to deal with the problem, short of outright nationalization, are rare. A response which one frequently gets in Italy in answer to the question as to why methods other than nationalization have not been tried is that Italian habits of lawlessness and disobedience would make it very unlikely that antitrust laws, on the American pattern, or other prohibitory or procedural legislation could or would be enforced. If the offending industry is simply nationalized, the problem of enforcement is removed. There is not yet much realization among Italians that the transfer of ownership from private to public hands does not necessarily bring an end to old abuses or prevent the appearance of new ones, as the history of ENI has amply proved.

Italy's antimonopoly tradition has been one of the primary contributors to keeping the Italian environment favorable to Mattei's and ENI's exercises of power. When added to the jingoist trait already discussed, it provided Mattei with a formidable weapon and an almost unassailable excuse. The antimonopoly tradition has had its greatest appeal among the educated and informed portions of the Italian population, a fact well known to Mattei. Many Italians who condemned Mattei for his highhanded, illegal, or vindictive behavior became, in the long run, his strongest defenders, on the ground that he and ENI constituted a great antimonopolistic force. (Whether Mattei's reputation in this regard is justified was a subject of discussion in Chapter 3.) Thus the antimonopoly tradition provided additional scope for Mattei's power by enlisting support, or at least neutrality, in quarters where he might otherwise have expected strenuous opposition. The antimonopoly theme also has had great appeal in the far-left segments of the Italian political rainbow, where "monopoly" and "private" tend to be equated; to these people, any attack on "monopoly" is also an attack on capitalism, NATO, and the Western Democracies. Mattei was well aware of the appeal possessed by the antimonopoly theme, and his public relations activities made skillful use of this knowledge. The annual reports, more likely to be read by the educated and informed, speak of ENI's antimonopoly mission in dignified and usually reasonable terms; on the other hand, newspaper interviews and radio and television statements have tended to be strident and extreme and usually have added antiforeign and antiprivate business texts to the antimonopoly theme.

Monopolies, real or imagined, were among Mattei's favorite and most useful straw men. They came to his defense when he defied the government; they increased his own monopoly power; they provided the spearhead of his attack on the international oil companies; they supported his ventures outside the field of hydrocarbons; they explained why some people opposed his policies; they were his excuses when he failed; they set his prices; they discovered the oil that he should have discovered; they were the dragons over which he, the little St. George, had to triumph. Were it not for their ghostly presence, Mattei's power would have been substantially impaired. In a country where "monopoly" has been blamed for every conceivable variety of economic and political ills, the artist who can skillfully play the tune of antimonopoly has a powerful force at his command.

The weak government—Power abhors a vacuum. "He [Mattei] could not be so strong if our government were not so weak," said an eminent Italian not long ago, thus putting his finger on what is perhaps the single most important aspect of the environment in which Mattei operated. The principle of relative power is nowhere better illustrated than in Mattei's situation in Italy at the time of his death. With no change other than an increase in the strength and stability of the Italian government, the whole ENI picture might have had to be redrawn. Certainly the descending curve of the strength of each succeeding postwar Italian government was matched by the ascending curve of Mattei's power and influence. In the early pre-ENI days of Mattei's reign, the government did have substantial, broad-based power and wide public support, but it was so preoccupied with other and much more important matters that Mattei was able to establish major beachheads of power even under a strong government. During the strong De Gasperi governments, nobody followed Mattei's actions very closely, and, furthermore, it would have taken remarkable will power to overcome the tremendous emotional impact which Mattei's discovery of the Po gas fields had upon the nation. On these beachheads, concealed by emotion and preoccupation elsewhere, Mattei built his power. As Christian Democratic majorities in Parliament decreased and finally disappeared altogether, the power vacuum in the government grew, and Mattei quickly and resolutely occupied it. The process accelerated rapidly after the death of Alcide de Gasperi. Government succeeded government without any of them having enough firm parliamentary support to assure continuity or adequate power to act on the many important issues facing the nation. The way was left open for Mattei to pursue his own course without danger of serious interference. The weaker and more precarious the government, the greater the leeway that was afforded to Mattei and ENI. As a result, Mattei enjoyed a sixteen-year period of a favorable power environment.

The recent *"apertura a sinistra,"* whereby the Nenni Socialists in exchange for certain concessions loosened their ties with the Communists and joined the government coalition, was hailed by people within ENI, including Mattei, as a harbinger of better things to come for ENI and for state ownership. Had Mattei really understood socialist dogma, he would not have been so optimistic about the *"apertura"* or so hopeful that it would improve ENI's position. Traditionally, socialist governments have maintained much closer control over their government corporations and agencies in the economic sector than have their capitalist counterparts. Around the world, there has been a tendency of socialist governments to prefer departmental administration and close political control of public enterprise, whereas the conservative governments seem to prefer the separate public corporation. Mattei, somehow, did not fit the pattern of the docile socialist bureaucrat who serves simply as an instrument of the government's own policies and carries out his orders without change or question. Should Nenni's Socialists come to have a major voice in

policy and to occupy cabinet positions in the government, both
of which they may now possess, ENI may find the government
demanding more advance consultation and more participation in
the activities of the Ente.

Mattei's ability, within the framework of a weak government, to
do pretty much as he pleased was only a part of the Mattei power
phenomenon in Italy. Not only was Enrico Mattei able to go his
own way, but he also on frequent occasion took Italy along with
him. Italian foreign policy in the Middle East has been largely
Mattei foreign policy since 1954, when he set out to redress the
alleged insult he had received from the Iran Consortium. A
Mattei-induced visit of President Gronchi to Iran no doubt played
an important part in ENI's precedent-breaking concession agreement with that country in 1957. The same can be said for Italian
policies in Africa, especially in Egypt, Libya, and Morocco. The
dedication of the ENI-Morocco refinery at Rabat in 1962 was
attended by a large portion of the Italian cabinet, which took the
opportunity to discuss Italian-Moroccan trade relations with officials of the Moroccan government. (Mattei himself did not
make the trip because of the attempted sabotage of his aircraft.)
Italian policy toward Yugoslavia has been affected by Mattei's
exploration agreement with that country. It is said in Italy that
the agreement with Yugoslavia had been signed before the Italian
cabinet knew anything about it. Mattei apparently was never officially authorized by the Italian government to approach the
USSR with regard to the purchase of crude oil and had completed
his arrangements before the government was informed. Each of
these acts manifests the extent of Mattei's power. None of these
acts would have been tolerated by a strong government.

Probably no Italian government in the last ten years could
have stood against determined Mattei opposition. So great was
his influence with his own party, and so popular was he with
the left, that only the most courageous or foolhardy of ministers
would have tried to pull up on Mattei's reins. The Segni government fell in 1960 because Malagodi and the Liberals made the
dumping of Mattei a condition of their continued support. This
is not to say, however, that there was any permanence in Mattei's

political position. His influence in the Christian Democratic Party probably was more secure than was his popularity with the far left. The Communists and Nenni Socialists supported him as long as it suited their purposes to do so, and found Mattei's antagonistic attitude toward private industry, both Italian and foreign, a convenient excuse for their endorsement. There are plenty of grounds on which they could, and occasionally did, oppose him. Only a slight shift of emphasis in the party line could have ended the honeymoon. The obvious ground for left-wing opposition, as the left fully realized, was that Enrico Mattei far more resembled a John D. Rockefeller or a Henry Ford than a submissive manager of a socialist state enterprise. But the fact remains that even without left-wing support Mattei still would have filled much of the power vacuum left by the weak government.

Sources of Mattei's Power

Not always easy to distinguish from the environmental factors surrounding Mattei's power are the wellsprings from which the power itself arose. The difference is more a matter of approach than of subject. From the way in which certain factors enhanced or protected or encouraged Mattei's power and its exercise, we shift our attention to the way in which these and other factors produced the power in the first place. Obviously, many factors could be examined legitimately in both connections, but it will not be necessary to do that here. In each approach, the significance of the other is reasonably clear. The economic position of ENI, for example, is both a source of power and a part of the environment which supports and enhances that power. What is more, other factors in the environment affect the method and the extent to which ENI's economic position can produce power.

Two major factors and several subsidiary factors are to be examined in connection with the so-called "sources" of power. The first major factor is Mattei himself. Just as a painting is created by the artist, not by the paint, so was Mattei's power largely created by Mattei, not by the materials he employed in obtaining his result. The second major factor, lack of account-

ability, is both a power-producing element employed by Mattei
in getting his finished product and also, at least in important part,
a creation of Mattei himself.

Enrico Mattei—Source of power and of danger. If any one
factor can be singled out as the most important element in the
fantastic growth of ENI and in the remarkable position of power
that Mattei held, that factor must be Enrico Mattei. Certainly,
without the other factors, the affairs of ENI and the power of
Mattei would not have developed as they did, but, almost as certainly, without Mattei, the affairs of ENI would not have developed at all. Only the unique combination of ingredients actually
present in Italy after World War II, including Mattei, can explain
the situation as we know it today. But only Mattei's personality,
skill, vigor, and singleness of purpose could have parlayed the
bankrupt shell of a Fascist azienda into the powerful international
corporation that is now ENI, and could have catalyzed the unpromising mix into a valuable product.

But this man is a paradox. Mattei was a master politician who
said he hated politics and politicians. He operated his business
in the best tradition of nineteenth-century capitalism but he attacked private business and was identified with the far left; he
has been called a "socialist robber baron." Mattei appeared publicly to dislike America, Americans, and American business
methods, yet hired American management consultants, copied
American service stations and motels, employed American technicians, used American public relations techniques, aped American
advertising methods, and much more nearly resembled a nineteenth-century American captain of industry than any modern
Italian businessman or public official. He had so little trust in
others that he held most of the key jobs in the entire ENI Group
himself, yet he hired editors for *Il Giorno* without much regard
for their qualifications or reliability. Mattei was thoroughly Italian and intensely nationalistic, but habitually ignored Italian customs and often condemned Italian traditions.

Through the paradox, however, shines the consistency of a
very pragmatic and very opportunistic man. He was extremely
skillful at achieving his ends by political means, when it was to

the advantage of ENI, but he deplored the machinations of politicians aimed at achieving ends which, to Mattei, seemed to have no value or which might thwart his own desires. He loved the accumulations of property and wealth, even though not for his personal estate, and enjoyed the power which these carried with them, although quick to condemn such motives in others. He was envious of American wealth and power, hated the oil companies that sought to block his aims in Italy and in the Middle East, and did not understand Anglo-Saxon ways of doing things, but this did not prevent him from recognizing methods and attributes which could be of use to him. So did Mattei recognize some of the facets of Italian character and some of the Italian customs and traditions which slowed the realization of his ambitions.

Mattei, if nothing else, was a realist. His enemies said he had no deep business principles, no code of ethics, no patterns of consistent behavior that lasted longer than from one moment of expediency to another, and even his friends said that he only did what was necessary in order to accomplish his ends. The real issue is: What were these ends that ruled his life, dominated ENI and influenced all of Italy? The only possible answer to this question is that some of the ends changed over the years and cannot always be determined with any degree of accuracy. Mattei's first objectives were probably no more than finding hydrocarbons in Italy, but when the natural gas was found in the Po Valley and when the pipelines were built or under way, Mattei raised his sights to sources of petroleum outside of Italy. After his first supposed rebuffs in Iran, vengeance on the offending oil companies became one of his aims. After that time, his motives included, separately and collectively: cheap sources of energy for Italy, regaining Italy's "natural" sphere of influence in the Mediterranean and in Africa, remaking the Italian economy, a new neo-Atlanticism, and always "power." This flexibility of object, when combined with a considerable flexibility of ethics, made for a very flexible man indeed.

Many of Mattei's methods were consistent with whatever motive or combination of motives happened at any given time to be dominant. The control of Christian Democrats in Parliament was useful no matter what Mattei might have been trying to do, and Mattei took no chances. Through fear and favor, Mattei acquired a substantial block of Deputies, how many it is impossible to tell. Estimates range as high as sixty. Friendship of reporters and the press was always valuable, and Mattei went far out of his way to get it. He was a devoted Catholic but did much more than most to assure the sympathy and support of the Church. He maintained close contacts with his old Partisan friends and with Partisan organizations. It is said that the only speeches Mattei enjoyed making were those given at the annual reunion of Partisan fighters.

Mattei had immense vitality and worked extremely hard. He was not of the consulting or the committee type. He usually devoted a great deal of thought to actions he was planning. Some of his employees were much irritated by his habit of springing suddenly on them topics to which he had devoted weeks of thought, and then being displeased when they did not on the spur of the moment analyze the topic as thoroughly as he had. Mattei gave all of his life to his work. He did little else, thought about little else, and talked about little else.

Mattei was intelligent, though even his friends sometimes say "shrewd" instead. With the limited knowledge and background he had, Mattei was able to do a great deal. He was a good judge of circumstances and situations, and he understood the Italian character completely. He was a doer and not a talker, who made decisions without waiting for every last scrap of evidence to be gathered. He played hunches and was very lucky. He could be aggressive and harsh when necessary, or gentle and patient. Mattei was a master of public relations techniques.

This unusual man combined his own talents with Italian national characteristics, a weak national government and an institutional independence of legal restraint, and created a power center which even Mussolini might have envied. Mattei made himself the most powerful man in Italy and his company one of the most important.

There have been other men like Mattei in modern history, both in industry and in government, and much of what has been said

about Mattei could be said about the others as well. The lover
of power is not a new phenomenon; Mattei was not the first op-
portunist. Men like Mattei are constantly moving across the pages
of history, but they make an impression on human events far
out of proportion to their numbers. All of these men have had
in common the attribute of being able to create and maintain
successful power relationships under a great variety of circumstances, some with personal prowess of body or mind, others
with wealth, and many with inherited position or rank. Like other
human beings, all have had defects of personality, of intelligence,
of motive, of education, or of training. Sometimes the defects
have actually served as assets, as where the reputation of a tyrant
for heartless cruelty may increase his power to gain his ends, or
where the defect exists in common with most of the public and
creates a bond of sympathy or understanding. Often the defect is
a source of danger to its possesser and to those around him. Whatever their nature or results, however, the defects form an integral
part of the power phenomenon and must be considered along
with the more positive factors.

Mattei's defects are not so easily discovered, enumerated, or
classified as his attributes, and very few Italians have even made
the attempt. In some ways, the effort is easier for an outsider,
who is less likely to permit the circumstances and the present
success to blot out the future and conceal the risks inherent in it,
and who is better able to penetrate assumptions and beliefs based
on personal involvement or indigenous public relations and propaganda. It is easy enough to condemn Mattei's unbridled power,
but power was not Mattei's weakness; power was only the instrument that made his defects dangerous. What we are called upon
to do is to examine these defects.

Mattei never read widely; he was not well educated; he had
little experience outside of Italy; and he was incapable of understanding ways of doing things and of looking at things other than
his own. His background, training, and outlook were very narrow. "A very unlettered man, he cannot even be called self-taught.
He knows next to nothing about modern history, literature, or
religion. He never reads a book and will only skim through certain

newspapers. His vocabulary is quite limited. Except on his own narrow subject, Mattei is most inarticulate." [29] Thus has Mattei been characterized, even by his friends.

Although his own corporation was a public one operating without government control, Mattei believed that the big international oil companies, including the American, were direct and conscious instruments of government policy. Many of his attacks on foreign oil companies in Italy were based on these assumptions. For many years, Mattei thought that Royal Dutch-Shell was an American company. Mattei's identification of himself with Italy and of his motives and policies with Italian motives and policies may help to explain why his own lack of supervision and control by the government did not loom large in his thinking, but it does not explain why he believed that Jersey Standard and Gulf were mere instrumentalities of the United States government. We can only assume that ignorance is the answer, but Mattei's being ignorant on a matter such as this is somewhat sobering to behold.

The gaps in Mattei's cultural, historical, and economic knowledge were huge. He made the mistake that so many have made before him of interpreting Anglo-Saxon standards of honesty, fair play, and trust as evidence of weakness and a sure sign that if you have fooled them once, you can do it again. He believed that Americans were naive in business and political matters and hence could be "taken." How he squared this with the hard facts he himself had run into in the oil industry is not clear. Mattei thought he understood the Arabs, as many other Italians have thought in the past, and did not realize that on several occasions he was being used by the Arabs as a means to their own ends. Perhaps misled by their support of him and his policies, Mattei also believed that he understood and could deal with the Communists and that they would continue to give him their support. One does not need to know Communists very well to know that this view was naive. They supported Mattei because his anti-American, antimonopoly, and antiprivate-business statements fitted well with the Communist line, but in supporting Mattei on these grounds the Communists had to ignore other, and probably more important, facets of Mattei which ran counter to Communist policy. Careful reading of the Italian Communist press made it all too clear that the Communists had not missed and had not forgotten these other facets. Mattei was often taken to task for his capitalistic behavior, for his support of the government, for his concern with profits, and for his failure to demand the nationalization of all industry. The Communists liked his Russian oil deal, his friendly relations with Nasser, his opposition to NATO and the Common Market and the turmoil Mattei caused in the international oil industry; but in doing so they had to overlook his close contacts with the Vatican, his independence of government supervision, and his great political power. Nobody knows how long Mattei's honeymoon with the far left would have continued, but many informed people in Italy now believe that the end was not far off when Mattei died. If it had come, it could not have helped but mark a decline in Mattei's power and influence.

Mattei's personality and his methods had a very deep and profound effect upon ENI and its organization. Although Mattei employed the services of one of the best American management consulting firms and heeded much of its advice, there were no significant changes in the organization at the top levels. At the time of Mattei's death, two men occupied all of the five top jobs in the ENI Group. In addition to being President of ENI, Mattei was president or director general of all the principal operating companies and of many of their subsidiaries.[30] Where Mattei was the chief executive officer, the next in actual position was almost invariably Ingegnere Girotti; where Mattei was not chief executive officer, Girotti usually was. The number of low-level management decisions that went all the way up to Girotti, or to Mattei, was very large. This situation would attract attention even if the ENI Group were small, but in a giant organization it is almost ludicrous. Mattei did not seem to appreciate the ramifications which ENI's rapid growth and great size had for his system of one-man rule. His subordinates had little influence on him or on his methods, though some of them occasionally made vigorous and sincere efforts to change his mind.

The ENI organization was on the verge of becoming an organism with a head and a body but with faulty communication between them. Because of his own great talents and because he had been at the head of the organization since its birth, Mattei still could keep considerable control over the details of his vast organization as it grew, but the day was rapidly approaching when no amount of skill, time, and knowledge would be enough to enable one man to handle all the aspects of the operation for which Mattei was responsible. Time will disclose the effects of Mattei's rule and his death.

The problem is much more difficult and more serious than one-man control, however. Not only was no attempt made to provide a successor for Mattei by giving other men broad experience across the wide spectrum of ENI's activities, but no effort was made even to acquaint the top operating men in the subsidiary companies with each other. There was no intercompany machinery of any kind except for Girotti and Mattei and some staff functions well below the top management of the operating companies. Mattei, personally, provided almost all of the centripetal force in the ENI Group. Now that Mattei has been removed from the scene, Girotti, the intercompany staff functions, and Mattei's successor, have little more than a fighting chance of holding the group tightly together. The explosion may yet be heard around the world. On top of all this, so strong was Mattei's influence that some of the operating heads aped Mattei and are conducting their own operations in the same fashion. Time after time, one operating chief or another was called to my attention by people in the ENI Group as being a "little Mattei" who never delegated, never consulted, and rarely convened his principal subordinates for any purpose whatsoever.

Though not primarily intended as such, this monograph cannot for several reasons avoid being a management study. In the first place, the kind and quality of the management have a great deal to do with the duration and scope of ENI as a power center. In the second place, the nature and extent of the power which Mattei and ENI wielded have had an effect upon the organization of the Group, its structure, its morale, and its performance. In the third place, one cannot understand Enrico Mattei and his position in Italy without a brief glimpse of the organization which he built and through which he worked.

The scope of the power which Mattei created for himself and for ENI, and through the exercise or collapse of which great dangers for Italy exist, is difficult to classify or describe. It penetrates the Italian economy through petroleum, fertilizers, rubber, metals, machinery, transportation, and also through government financial policy, as the more than 228 billion lire in outstanding government guaranteed long-term bonded indebtedness makes only too clear. Mattei's power penetrated the government in almost all branches and at all levels; Mattei was, for all practical purposes, a minister without portfolio in areas as widely diverse as foreign relations, finance, commerce and industry, state participations, nuclear power, agriculture, treasury, and the general accounting office.

Lack of accountability. Important as Mattei himself was in the development of the great power that he wielded, other contributions cannot be ignored. It must be admitted that many of the other sources of Mattei's power were stimulated or developed, at least in part, by Mattei, but now make substantial contributions of their own. Most significant among these is the absence of statutory and other formal restraints on ENI and its president. The fact is that Mattei really was accountable to no one. Part of this situation was the result of Mattei's own doing; part of it was the result of the confused state of Italian law with regard to public corporations; and part can be attributed to the unwillingness of government officials to stick their necks out. Some of the machinery for enforcing accountability is in existence in Italy, but there is little precedent for its use.

Much of the machinery has been perverted to the point where it runs in reverse and serves as a means for the public agency to accomplish its own ends, rather than as an instrument of government control. The Ministry of State Participations, for example, was an institution employed by Mattei to mouth his own principles and objectives, to lend an air of legitimacy to his activities, and to provide an appearance of supervision and control by the government. Those not in the know were unaware of the fact that most of the directives of the Ministry, which Mattei so obsequiously obeyed, were influenced by Mattei in accordance with his own intentions and desired ends. So, when ENI's annual report states that certain action has been taken "in response to directives of the Ministry," one usually may translate this sentence to mean that Mattei already had taken the action and wanted some support for it, or that Mattei wanted to take the action but thought, for public relations or other reasons, that it would be wiser to act under the aegis of the Ministry. The Minister's now famous Program Report of 1961, which purports to set forth official government policy in support of state intervention in Italy's economic affairs, undoubtedly was influenced and approved by Mattei himself, and it made a very nice framework within which Mattei could justify and explain his actions.

The presence of representatives from the various ministries on ENI's internal governing boards also made it appear as though ENI and Mattei were under constant government surveillance. Actually, these men were never consulted, were rarely informed, and depended for most of their information on Mattei's own public relations announcements. The delegate of the Court of Accounts appeared to have the responsibility of checking the report of the Board of Auditors and ENI's financial statements, thus greatly improving the atmosphere of control and audit by responsible government officials. As a matter of fact, "signing" the reports and statements was just about the sum total of the activity required of the delegate.

In a free society, a public corporation creates a paradox. With too little control, accountability, and responsibility, its power raises threats of tyranny and of the weakening of democratic institutions; with too much, it becomes the tool of political whimsy and no longer can perform the tasks for which it was brought into existence. In a well-intended effort to avoid one horn of the dilemma, one enterprise often is impaled upon the other. The public corporation is neither so venerable nor so well understood that much guidance can be found in experience. Some of the boundaries have been located, and some of the basic principles enumerated, but beyond those achievements there is little that can be said with certainty. Experience has varied considerably from country to country and from corporation to corporation, and most national legislative bodies have failed to maintain consistent policies over periods of time sufficiently long to provide useful information and experience.

Italy has long employed public corporations to accomplish ends thought to be desirable, and a body of literature has grown up in that country around the public corporation, its nature, functions, and problems. As a matter of fact, the Italian literature today shows a much better understanding of modern public companies than it does of modern private ones. This result is due in part to the Italian tendency to deal with disruptions, monopolistic conditions, and vagaries in the private sector of the economy by nationalizing the industries or companies affected. The sad fact is, however, that few useful principles can be extracted from the Italian experience or literature. The Italian companies, except in outline, conform to no particular pattern and follow no particular rule or form. They all carry the trademarks of their environment at the time of creation. Some are pre-Fascist, many date from the Fascist period, and some came into existence after World War II. Many were organized hastily and with little thought or planning; others have been the subject of years of study and debate. Some occupy sectors of the economy that are traditionally of a public nature; others are operating in largely private fields and in competition with private companies. On top of these variations, the Parliament has piled frequent changes of form and altered rules of behavior.

As a group, the Italian public corporations have been subject to a bewildering array of checks, controls, audits, reporting responsibilities, and political interference. In some cases, the array was so involved and complicated that it provided a protective screen for the corporation, which operated very much as it pleased. It was in this confused atmosphere that ENI saw the light of day. Although extensive studies, investigations, and hearings on the public corporation were at the time underway, the ENI statute bears the imprint of the then existing situation. The imprint is made evident in two very different ways. In the first, the form of the company is the traditional one, with the usual boards and councils and committees and the usual representation from among the ministries. In the second way, however, we see the attempts on the part of the draftsmen of the ENI statute (reputedly Mattei, who was at that time still a member of the National Assembly, and Minister Ezio Vanoni) to avoid the troublesome controls, responsibilities, and interference to which other public companies had been subjected. In these attempts lies a major source of ENI's power.

The cornerstone of ENI's independence of the government is the lack of auditing procedures. The forms are there, but the substance is not. The Collegio Sindacale, which appears in most Italian corporations, public and private, is present also in ENI. But this curious institution, the chairman of which, in public companies, is a representative of the General Accounting Office, is concerned primarily with internal control and in no sense performs an external or independent auditing function. The details of its functions are spelled out in the *Codice civile* and in the charter of the particular corporation, but, in the case of ENI, these functions are almost completely sterile. The Collegio reports to nobody in particular; lines of authority are not clearly established; and there is no individual or officer who is required to read the reports of the Collegio or listen to its entreaties. Mattei's powerful personality functioned beautifully in this confused atmosphere.

Article 19 of the ENI law provides another bit of impressive, but sterile, control machinery. Under that Article, the president, the board of directors and the executive committee of the Ente all can be removed, "in the event of serious irregularity," by decree of the President of the Republic, on the recommendation of the Ministers of State Participations, Treasury, *and* Industry and Commerce. The requirement of unanimity among the three ministers, the determination of "serious irregularity," and the reluctance of public officials to stick their necks out have been very good insurance against the use of Article 19. Were the study of ENI's accountability confined to a perusal of the statutes and the codes, it would be logical to conclude that the machinery of

government control was not just adequate but excessive. The look
below the surface shows exactly the opposite to be true, a fact
to which a large part of Mattei's power can be traced.

This being the case, it might be asked whether the same conclusions can be drawn with regard to other Italian public companies. Obviously, the same set of basic conditions operate upon
them, but the answer to the question must be a reasonably assured "no." None of the other public companies had Mattei; and
none of the others was designed to make fullest use of the in-
tricacies and confusions of the situation. ENI did not "just grow";
ENI was planned and organized with a particular result in mind.
The aura of responsibility was retained, but the substance, of
which there was not very much anyhow, was eliminated. By
centralizing the organization of ENI and by neglecting the
procedures of audit, Mattei achieved the independence he wanted.

Limits of Mattei's Power

In order fully to comprehend the scope of the power possessed
by Mattei and ENI, it is necessary to examine briefly some of the
details of its outer boundaries and to shift our attention, for a
moment, from the nature, source, and manifestations of the power
to its limits. An effort along these lines is desirable, also, before
we attempt to reach any final conclusions or to make useful
predictions for the future. Finally, a measure of concentration
upon the limits of power often will help to reveal certain attributes
of that power which might otherwise be concealed from our view.
Many of the recent studies of the large American corporation as
an economic, social, and political phenomenon have devoted considerable attention to the issue of limits on power, both in terms
of existing limits and of evolving limits. Our discussion here may
make possible some interesting comparisons.

Some of the power limits to be considered are of universal application; others have particular relevance to ENI or to Italy.
Some are obvious, some subtle, some highly speculative. The list
of limits can by no means be exhaustive, not only because of the
relatively minor importance of some, but also because new limitations have arisen since Mattei's death. Our discussion will be con-

fined, with a few minor exceptions, to the situation as it existed while Mattei was in control of ENI.

If we were discussing a large American private corporation, we might begin our list of limitations with the overriding power of the state, which, when in open conflict with a private business corporation, is always capable of exerting superior force and imposing its will. Whether it *will* exert such force is another issue. We may begin our treatment of limitations upon ENI's power at the same point, but with somewhat different conclusions. Measured in terms of tanks, guns and soldiers, the Italian state always commanded greater force than Mattei and ENI, but in terms of political power capable of exerting and maintaining any kind of force with regard to ENI, the answer was very much in doubt. As was said elsewhere, no recent Italian government could be assured of winning a showdown with Mattei, whose support from the large and powerful ranks of the far left, from a large block in the Christian Democratic Party itself, from the Church and from the press gave him such power that only a clear-cut issue of Mattei versus ITALY could definitely have shifted the balance away from Mattei. Although the overriding power of the Italian state would have come into operation at some point, the range of activity left to Mattei was vast, as events have proved. Short of clear, deep, and dangerous issues of national importance, the power of the Italian state was not an effective limitation on Mattei and ENI. This conclusion is somewhat of a paradox in itself, inasmuch as ENI is legally an instrumentality of the very state which possessed inadequate power to control it.

There was nothing inherently permanent about the above conditions, however, and they can be said to have been applicable only in the short run. For the long run, several reservations must, obviously, be made. In the first place, the government might have increased in strength. Fanfani's tremendous effort to persuade his own party to accept the "*apertura a sinistra*" and the party's eventual acceptance of the policy, were based largely on the twofold objective of breaking the ties between the Communists and the Nenni Socialists, and of strengthening the power of the government in office. It is still too early to tell whether these objectives will be attained. There are serious doubts. There is little evidence that the uncompromising factions in the Christian Democratic Party itself can be held together forcefully enough to maintain a strong government, but had a strengthening taken place during Mattei's tenure, the extent of his power and the scope of ENI's operation would have been reduced. The same can be said of the existing ENI power center, although it must be recognized that without Mattei that power center is only a shadow of its former self.

Although the "opening to the left" may not have substantially increased the power of the government generally, there are at least two possibilities of increased government power with regard to ENI. The Socialists may use their new influence to bring ENI into conformance with the traditional socialist pattern of the responsible commissariat and to alter the circumstances under which ENI has been permitted to behave as though it were a highly privileged private corporation. On another score, too, additional restraints on Mattei's power might have been built: If the Communists, for reasons of their own, had decided to remove their support from Mattei, his strength would have been substantially lessened relative to the government. Had the far left press attacked Mattei vigorously, the myth of his infallibility might have been, to some extent at least, dispelled. Even Mattei's remarkable public relations skills would have found it difficult to overcome the opposition of a large segment of the public press. Under circumstances where Mattei's power was weakened, in absolute terms, the power of the state might have been sufficient to check that of Mattei and ENI.

An ultimate limit on the power of ENI was Mattei's own mortality. As is amply clear by this time, the power of ENI was largely personal to Mattei and without him must necessarily drop to a much lower level. Were the top management of ENI organized differently and had there been heirs apparent in the scheme of things, Mattei's lifespan might not have marked the limits of ENI's extraordinary power. Mattei's power and ENI's power cannot be considered separately, and with Mattei's death departed the power wielded by the man and much of the power wielded by the organization. The sudden dissipation of power in this fashion may, itself, be destructive, just as the recession of the water after a tidal wave may be as dangerous as the wave itself. Other power centers may find themselves relatively more powerful than before and rush to fill the vacuum.

The market place is a traditional regulator of power. An interesting aspect of the large American corporation in modern society has been the apparent decline of the market place as a restraint on power. It has not disappeared, and will not disappear, but its effects are different and less marked. The market place acts in two principal ways as a restraint on power: competition for capital and competition for custom. ENI has had strong rivals in both contests. In the former, they are domestic rivals, in the latter, foreign. ENI has had little difficulty in finding necessary capital. The vast size and diversity of the ENI organization now makes possible considerable intercompany financing even beyond the Po gas, and the political power enjoyed by ENI has given it certain privileges and advantages in the capital markets not attainable by others. If ENI finds "big oil" in the Middle East or in Africa, additional sources of funds may become available. The Po profits depend on several factors: the lack of competitive substitutes, political forces which permit ENI to price its natural gas far above its costs, political power which protects ENI from audit, and, of course, the continued supply of gas. Present levels of production seem likely to continue for ten to twelve years; effective competition is not in sight, except in the long run (atomic energy). The importance of the political influence has been discussed thoroughly already.

ENI's present sources of capital have been adequate for most needs, but the Po profits probably have reached maximum levels; the public borrowing cannot go on indefinitely without having adverse effects on the Ente; and besides, because Mattei denied so often any reliance on the public treasury, a government subsidy is not likely. Failure to find "big oil" within two or three years may seriously impair the availability of capital and certainly would weaken the Ente's public support, and the same would have been true even if Mattei had survived.

In spite of large and powerful rivals, Mattei had also been winning the competition for custom. That he was able to do so can be attributed to a number of factors, some of which were not available to his competitors. In the first place, he appealed to the patriotic and nationalistic character of the Italians. The AGIP gasoline, Supercortemaggiore, is always advertised as "The Powerful *Italian* Gasoline," for example, and we already are familiar with Mattei's chauvinistic attacks on the "foreign" oil monopoly. The other Italian oil companies are so small as to be of little relevance to our discussion. Mattei constructed a sword of Damocles over the heads of his foreign competition by threats of nationalization. He is reputed to have told Jersey Standard, when it balked at refining his difficult Egyptian crude in ENI's and Esso's jointly owned Italian refineries, that "If you don't refine it, we will just nationalize you." This threat may account, at least in part, for the failure of foreign competitors to invest huge sums in Mattei style motels and super service stations.

In price competition, gasoline is down to the point where the foreign competitors seem to be losing money on that product and where AGIP probably is losing money too. The cheap Russian oil (politically priced, as his opponents charge) made it possible for Mattei to compete effectively with the large foreign oil companies who had access to Middle East oil. AGIP's share of the Italian market has been steadily increasing and now approaches 30 per cent. Mattei may have considered the small loss on gasoline to be a sound investment in terms of the goodwill of the increasingly numerous Italian motorists and for the purpose of keeping his foreign competitors off balance and unenthusiastic about the Italian market. Mattei's leverage here would have increased had he found "big oil."

Even outside of Italy, Mattei still was an effective competitor despite the lack of major advantages enjoyed at home. Often his competitive activities were based wholly or largely on political grounds, as in Morocco and some other parts of Africa, but they were just as often based on sound economic grounds of price or service. One of Mattei's most interesting ventures outside of Italy was his invasion of Great Britain with retail gasoline. In spite of his denials that he planned a program of price cutting, the only possible way for ENI to obtain and keep a foothold in the British market would have been by price competition with the major oil companies already dominating that market. Mattei had a sharp eye for the high-margin markets, and picked Great Britain as a likely target, not only on economic grounds but also for the purpose of administering the stiletto to three of his favorite enemies (British Petroleum, Shell, and Jersey Standard). It has been rumored since Mattei's death, however, that ENI will abandon its efforts in Britain. Outside of Italy and the Communist or Communist-sympathizing countries, competition from the other international oil companies was and is an effective check on the power of ENI. For most practical purposes, the boundaries of Italy, except for nuisance or mischief value, were also the geographical limits of Mattei's power. Once outside Italy, other power centers became both numerous and strong and, therefore, reduced ENI's relative power to a low level. Even its nuisance value in the international petroleum industry may decline if ENI strikes "big oil" and finds itself facing the same problems confronting the other major oil companies.

Among the potential checks on Mattei, even inside Italy, was the Common Market. Mattei did not approve of the Common Market and opposed Italy's membership. He made it plain that he did not understand the significance of the mass market on an international scale. He accused Americans of being naive for supporting the Common Market concept in Europe. Although he mellowed somewhat in later years, Mattei always seemed to see even his own markets abroad through nationalistic eyes. He probably also saw the Common Market as a weakening influence on his nationalistic approach to trade and a threat to some of the barriers that protected his flanks in Italy, not only with regard to petroleum but in many of the other fields in which ENI was active. One important contribution to ENI's climb to power was the fact that Italy was not presented with any clear alternatives in viable or salable form. The Common Market probably will

supply new alternatives. Had Great Britain been admitted to the
Common Market during Mattei's lifetime his power position
would probably have been weakened.

The last boundary here to be discussed is that of public opinion.
Under ordinary circumstances, it is not an effective check on
economic power. Public opinion is usually slow to act and then
is often extreme in its scope. Major changes are very difficult to
predict or control. There is no doubt that the climate of public
opinion in Italy was, and still is, very favorable to Mattei and ENI.
This was in part due to Mattei's own public relations efforts, but
some of the favor he enjoyed must be attributed to factors such
as nationalistic pride, real economic benefits, and a traditional
predilection for nationalized industry and acceptance of extralegal
conduct, all of which constituted a firm foundation for continued
public support. There were weaknesses in the picture, however,
as has been pointed out. Mattei's public relations program would
have been considerably shaken had the political far left and its
rather substantial share of the press removed its support from him
or begun actively to attack him. The economic benefits already
being enjoyed may fade in importance unless joined by new ones.
The present low price of gasoline may not appear in the same
attractive light when the older and higher prices are forgotten.

Mattei made mistakes, any one of which, if effectively employed against him, could considerably have dimmed his reputation for intelligence and infallibility, and had he lived, he undoubtedly would have made more mistakes. For example, *Il
Giorno* was a potential source of danger to him, though he seemed
not to realize it. The editor's mistake might soon have become
Mattei's mistake. Public opinion can shift very quickly, and the
shifts are often particularly violent when induced by disillusionment or the feeling that the public has been duped.

POWER THEORY AND POWER PRACTICE

Most of the foregoing section was based upon the conceptual
framework of power described at the beginning of this chapter,

but no great effort was made to test the validity of the concept directly against the observable phenomena surrounding ENI and Mattei. If a modern concept of power can eventually be used as a tool of research and analysis in connection with power phenomena, we should be able here to make some preliminary forays into the area.

It probably is obvious enough that the traditional concepts of power do not throw much light on the ENI situation in Italy. Naked power occasionally can be discerned, but to set up naked power as the focus of our study would be fatal to our objectives; there would not be very much to talk about, and most phenomena would have to go unexplained. The "ruler and the ruled" approach would be still less useful; even the two key words have misleading connotations. The concept which is based on the assumption that power is necessarily evil forces us either to the irrational policy of eradication of power or to the frustrating conclusion that one of society's major mechanisms is bad but has to be employed in order to achieve good objectives. Ethical, religious, and moralistic concepts of power are not very helpful in power analysis, except as supplements to sociological or psychological approaches, but they do play a role in long-run attempts to control power; they are also significant in terms of national beliefs and traits which affect the scope and exercise of power. Some of the traditional concepts are inconsistent with each other. Even if we combined those which possessed consistent or complementary factors, we still would find ourselves without a usable concept. For this reason, a modern concept has been evolved, and for this reason also we devote a little more time to seeing whether that concept fits the observed phenomena. In the pages to follow, we shall test not only the three basic characteristics of our modern concept of power but also some of the subsidiary or collateral elements.

Basic Characteristics of the Power Concept

Power as a relationship. It would be impractical to attempt to analyze all the power relationships in which Mattei and ENI were involved. It is sufficient, in order to test our concept, to examine only a few of the more important ones. The most important of them, and the most interesting, is Mattei's relationship with the Italian government.

Were we to begin our investigation with the usual chart of government organization or of the chain of responsibility, we would see the Parliament, with its ultimate responsibility and authority in most matters, at the top. The Cabinet, to which Parliament and the Constitution assign executive and administrative functions, would be next in line; basic public policies would be implemented here through directives to the various ministers who make up the Cabinet and to their ministries. Broad policies affecting public companies would be interpreted largely in the Ministry of State Participations, and guidelines for compliance with these policies would be established and made known to the public companies through their responsible officers and boards; the Ministries of Finance, the Treasury, and Industry and Commerce would play collateral roles in this function. Whenever questions arose within the Ente itself as to the appropriateness of certain contemplated action or policy one of the ministries might have to be consulted, or perhaps even the Cabinet or the Parliament. Without devoting too much time to details, it can be said that government policy would be brought to bear upon the public companies from the top down, and that the public companies would appear at the lower levels of the hierarchy of power. If this outline accurately described Mattei's situation, our attention would have to be focused on relationships like those between him and his customers and suppliers, between him and other oil companies, and between him and the public. The relationship between Mattei and the government would be of interest primarily from the standpoint of Mattei as a "wieldee" rather than a "wielder" of power.

We know from experience that real power situations are never as simple as the outline above and that, in the case of Mattei, the inverse hierarchy might actually be more accurate. Mattei's relationship with his government was much more nearly that of the wielder of power than the other way around, though, clearly, it is not exclusively the one or the other. To say that Mattei had power with respect to the government is only slightly more useful than saying that the government had power with respect to Mattei. Both statements are true and both are false unless one carefully specifies the circumstances. To a greater or lesser degree, these observations would be applicable to any power relationship. The scope, and even the nature, of power are influenced reciprocally. The reactions of the subordinate party to the power sought to be exercised over him are an important part of the power phenomenon and also serve to influence the character and the extent of the power sought to be exercised. The person or group in the subordinate position always has some power, albeit sometimes negative or offsetting in character, and, under some circumstances, may actually be in a superior position. An employee, for example, normally will have a subordinate position with respect to his employer, under the circumstances of his employment, but may have a superior position under the circumstances of a lodge, social club, or military reserve unit. A subordinate government agency may actually wield power under some circumstances, over its own ministry or department, as a result of superior knowledge, intrenched position with regard to some person or group superior to both, or the like. It is obvious, however, that none of these relatively normal situations serves to describe Mattei's relationship to his government.

Mattei's subordinate position on the organization chart was borne out hardly at all in practice. There might have been some issues with regard to which the government could have made a superior appeal to public opinion, and thus might have been able to wield power greater than Mattei's on those issues, but, generally speaking, Mattei wielded more power than did the government in most of the areas in which he was interested. Although usually capable of being related in some way to hydrocarbons, these areas of interest extended from domestic economic policy to foreign policy. Without doubt, the government had great power in matters of foreign policy, but not in relation to Mattei in the areas which he had invaded. Italian foreign policy in Africa and the Middle East is now essentially Mattei foreign policy. But it is important to note that Mattei was well enough aware and appreciative of the public image of his power relationship with the government that he went out of his way to maintain the fiction that he was the public servant who obediently took orders rather than giving them. Mattei realized, no doubt, that his power would have been measurably weakened had he intentionally destroyed or allowed to be dispelled, the traditional image.

But what of the relationship that made this unusual situation possible? In the first place, Mattei's power relationship with his government was established during a period when the attention of the government was directed elsewhere or blinded by the cloud of gas rising out of the Po fields. Mattei at that time began to make decisions affecting the government's own policies and to occupy strategic positions from which later and weaker governments were to find it impossible to dislodge him. By the time it could begin to devote attention to Mattei, the government was too precarious to do anything about the situations it found and quickly returned to its position of hearing and seeing no evil. So long as Mattei was willing to create an appearance of consulting with his government and obeying its directives—an illusion which his public relations policies dictated anyway—the government was only too happy not to face a showdown or a direct test of power.

In the second place, the relationship between Mattei and the government was directly influenced by Mattei's relationship with Parliament. The Cabinet not only faced Mattei but also had to guard against his forays from the rear. Mattei had been the source of so much financial support for so many Christian Democratic Deputies for so long that he appeared to have more influence with the governing party than did its nominal heads. In the third place, Mattei had access to public relations skills and techniques that the government could not match. He bought newspaper support or neutrality across the entire range of journalistic opinion and could always count on a large and sympathetic forum for the expression of his side of any issue.

Last, but most important, a large segment of the government genuinely supported Mattei's policies, agreed with his views, and wished that it could have done what he had done. There are many government officials in Italy who saw Mattei as the embodiment of the strength which the government itself did not have. He was free of the parliamentary bickering, of the frustrating facts of life with which a coalition government must live, of the need for keeping America, NATO, and the Common Market countries contented. He could call a spade a spade, or pluck the eagle's tail feathers, twist the lion's tail, tease the French or deal with the Russians without being punished. He could fly about in his own jet airplane, build modern glass skyscrapers, refuse to hire politicians' nephews, buy newspapers, and rehabilitate cities without having to face the ire of antiquarians or Hottentots. The fact is that Mattei and his power were partly a reflection of the Italian political and economic climate and the frustrations and emotions which beset it. Mattei did what many in the government think should have been done. I believe, too, that there is a deep respect among Italians for the strong, aggressive, independent personality. A man like Mattei is widely admired and envied. Government officials are not immune to these feelings. Mattei's relationship with the government was profoundly influenced by a willingness to overlook deviations as the price of achieving common goals. Again, the importance of the reciprocal reactions between the power wielder and the power wieldee is emphasized.

Though the most important and the most interesting, Mattei's power relationship with the government was not the only power relationship in which he played the dominant role. The industrial users of ENI's natural gas, some of them among the largest private industrial firms in Italy, submitted to Mattei's pricing scheme with few complaints. What is more, they rarely showed any public concern over Mattei's refusal to release estimates as to the reserves in the Po fields, and they almost never replied when Mattei accused them of being price-gouging monopolists or greedy exploiters of the masses or promoted their nationalization. They did not even have much to say when Mattei used the profits from the gas he sold to them to build petrochemical installations producing competitive products, as he did with fertilizer and Montecatini. Many of the same forces acting to create and maintain the unusual relationship between Mattei and the government also acted upon the relationship with Italy's large private industry. The threat of nationalization, made viable by Mattei's influence in the government, led many private industrialists to avoid open conflict with Mattei. Others were deterred from actions that might antagonize Mattei by fear of other types of retribution. It also is easy to find Italian businessmen who supported and admired Mattei for what he was able to do in Italy, for the prestige and respect he obtained for Italy abroad, and for his nationalistic policies and pronouncements. Mixed feelings of fear and admiration seem to have contributed to a rather stable power relationship.

The relationship with the foreign oil companies operating in Italy was unlike the other two relationships which have been discussed. These companies had firsthand experience with Mattei's power. They were officially excluded from the Po Valley in 1953 and from exploration in the rest of Italy by the Oil Law of 1957, and one of them had felt the hot breath of Mattei's ability to stir up the far left against it in Sicily. They had watched Mattei cut the already low price of gasoline to a point where the product was scarcely profitable, and do it under the guise of breaking the stranglehold of the foreign monopolists and eliminating their monopoly profits. Standard of New Jersey learned what it was like to be a refining partner of a man who could probably make good on his threats to have them nationalized if they balked at refining his salty crude from Egypt or his political crude from Russia. But, seemingly in an effort to give Mattei additional ammunition against them, they continued to behave toward Mattei in the heavy-handed, arrogant way which was certain to keep public opinion and the power relationship stacked in Mattei's favor. Instead of fighting Mattei with economic weapons, which they commanded in much greater strength than he, they persisted in trying to fight him with political and propaganda pressures, his own weapons, which he turned against them.

Power as a dynamic quantity. The ENI situation in Italy is one of the best sources of evidence that power is not static in amount but is constantly in flux, being produced, weakened, strengthened, or destroyed. Most of Mattei's power was produced by him and not extracted from someone else. The Po gas fields produced new power, economic, social, and political, and stimulated the production of further power in the users of the gas and in the Italian economy as a whole. The new Italian economic power was not torn from the mutilated corpse of another power wielder but was largely produced anew. In one sense, certainly, some of Mattei's power existed at the expense of the power of the Italian government, but I am not convinced that the quantity of such usurped power was extensive. Though part of the power of the government did accrue to Mattei, the growth in his power was not a principal cause of the decline of the government's power, and a large portion of the power which Mattei wielded was power that the Italian government never had. Can it be said that, if there had been no Mattei and no ENI, the power of the government would now be greater? Probably not. It is no exaggeration to say that the new economic power created by Mattei actually increased the power of the Italian government, except in relation to Mattei himself, over what it would have been without him.

There is little doubt but that Mattei's power altered power relationships in all aspects of Italian society, reducing power here, usurping power there, and creating power in another place; but the total amount of power appears to have been substantially increased. In renewed confidence alone, Italy now has vastly more power with which to attack its economic and social problems and to offset its natural disadvantages. Perhaps it could be argued that the power was there all along but only needed to be organized and mobilized. This approach bears too close a resemblance to some of the old ideas of natural law, which held law to be in existence but in need of discovery, to be attractive today. It is probably more useful to think of power as coming into existence through production out of the raw materials of society than it is to view it as a substance that requires discovery and resurrection.

Power as a resource of society. In order to avoid conflict with the conclusion that power, like wealth, is not static in quantity but is constantly being produced, we must state the third characteristic of our power concept as follows: power and the capacity to produce it, like wealth and the capacity to produce wealth, are resources of society which can be used to benefit society and to aid in solving some of the problems of society.

In this sense, power, like wealth, can be organized and mobilized for the benefit of society, as well as for its detriment. The traditional, and still rather common, view that power is necessarily evil prevents further analysis of power and forecloses the use for society's benefit of one of society's most valuable tools.

Mattei used the power created by his reputation as a Partisan leader to disobey the government's order to liquidate and to build the pipelines in the face of overwhelming obstacles. Thus were resources of power employed to begin the alleviation of Italy's historic shortage of energy. Mattei then mobilized his own political power, the economic power produced by the natural gas, and the confidence and optimism beginning to appear in Italy to get the gas to market, to extract substantial profits that could be used for further exploration and for excursions into related fields, and to do other things, some of which were not necessarily for the greater good of Italy. Had it not been for these uses of power, Italy's modern miracle might never have taken place.

Most of the events described in the previous paragraph were, of course, unplanned, but fortuitous mobilizations of power may be as beneficial to society as the planned variety. Mattei did not know that he would find large gas deposits at Cortemaggiore and certainly did not predict the fantastic economic expansion that would take place in Italy, but he did have as one of his objectives a solution of Italy's energy shortage. His power and his understanding of the uses of power made it possible for him to do what no one else, not even the government, could have done at that time. The fact that he did not consciously mobilize the power as he would mix cement, sand, and water does not detract from the concrete value of the result or from the conclusion that power is a resource of society. Obviously, not all of Mattei's power was exercised for the benefit of society, and Mattei was subject to censure for this, but the accomplishments speak for themselves. Unfortunately, the credit side of the ledger has not shown much of a gain outside the Po gas and a few other less important entries. As Mattei's power increased, the beneficial results became harder and harder to identify. Much of the power seems to have been wasted on useless or even harmful ends.

Other Characteristics of the Power Concept

Power is agglutinative. Mentioned briefly in the early parts of this chapter was the observation that the wielder of one form of power tends to acquire other forms of power also. In 1946, Mattei's power was based almost exclusively on his reputation as a Partisan organizer, but, as the years went by, he came into possession of many other forms of power as well. Economic power was soon added to his portfolio; power over opinion came very early and was long one of the most important; power behind the scenes, Russell's classification,[31] was also part of Mattei's repertoire; political power, of several varieties, was added early and was continuously augmented. Within the framework of Weber's classification of power,[32] it can be said that Mattei's power was basically charismatic in character, on the ground that most persons and groups in the subordinate positions submitted because of their belief in the extraordinary quality of the power holder and in the ends which he advocated; but traditional power also played its part as a result of Mattei's extensive contributions to Church, party, and to individual politician or officeholder; and in some areas legal power can be identified in the statutes granting monopoly rights in exploration and production.

Power is hierarchical. Of even greater validity today than in ancient times, when it was first put forward, is the observation that power is never a matter of the many ruled by the one, but is instead a hierarchy of power relationships. To a large extent, Mattei's power was made up of his own personal attributes, but none of these attributes was the kind that operates without the coöperation of other persons and groups. Mattei's primary attribute was his ability to create and to use power hierarchies. The success with which Mattei impressed his views on the Italian government cannot be laid at the door of his commanding presence or great physical strength, because he really possessed neither of these characteristics. It is in fact attributable to a vast and complicated array of power hierarchies and power relationships operating through the ENI organization, through the press and Parliament, through the ministries and civil servants, and through political parties and the Church, each level of the hierarchies and each of the power relationships depending on different combinations of power elements, including personal attributes, economic power, and sympathy with Mattei's expressed objectives or methods.

Paradox of power. It was suggested at the beginning of this chapter that, paradoxically, power appears to be most secure when it is not under the necessity of showing itself in the form of naked force. Because Mattei had no army and no guns, he could not employ physical force even if he were challenged, but Mattei had at his command other types of force which could have been utilized if the challenge had actually taken place. His ability to remove financial support from large numbers of politicians, his ability to stir the far left into action and his apparent ability to bring down the government were all matters of naked power. The remarkable thing was that the challenges to Mattei were so few and so weak. Never was he really called upon for more than a casual threat of force, which, of course, was a tribute to the depth and the scope of his power. There is no intention here to imply that Mattei could have resisted any challenge that might have been hurled at him. It is only being asserted that the security of Mattei's power was borne out by the absence of challenge and by the lack of any need to exercise force. There were some potential challenges that might very well have defeated Mattei. Among these were the weaknesses in his economic power and the increased influence in the government of the far-left political parties.

Ideas and power. There is little need at this point, except for purposes of emphasis, to repeat the conclusion that ideas and beliefs are important to the production, maintenance, and exercise of power. We have described in some detail the significance to Mattei's power of certain national traits. Traditions of lawlessness, jingoism, and vanity shaped his power, extended its scope, and influenced the way in which it was exercised. Religious beliefs also affect power. Were Italians of the Buddhist faith, there probably never would have been a Mattei. What a person believes influences both the way in which he exercises power and the way in which he reacts to its exercise by others. Mattei made skillful use of this simple observation, as has already been discussed.

Measurement of power. The state of the art has not yet advanced to the point where power can be measured with any degree of accuracy. Experience has taught us how very inaccurate even relative superiority in tanks and troops and warheads is as a measure of power. Lasswell's approach [33] through the degree of participation in the making of decisions is as useful a guide as any now in existence. If we use extreme care, it is possible under some circumstances to say that with regard to decision "x," Jones at this moment has more power than Smith. This, in effect, is what already has been done in our discussion of Mattei's power. With regard to exploration and production in the field of hydrocarbons in Italy, Mattei had more power than the government. In decisions affecting Italian foreign policy in the Middle East and North Africa, under then existing conditions, Mattei appears to have had superior power. In decisions affecting Italian policy in the Common Market, however, the government certainly had greater power than Mattei.

Mattei participated in decisions across a very wide spectrum. With regard to most of these decisions, we could draw carefully qualified conclusions as to Mattei's or ENI's power, along the lines suggested above. Each conclusion would be, then, an approximation of Mattei's relative power under the described set of circumstances, but it is not at all clear that this approach would be of any value in making predictions for the future. However, under present conditions, Lasswell's technique [34] is useful in power research and analysis, and it is to be expected that with increased understanding of power will come the tools through which power phenomena may be better utilized, controlled, and forecast for the benefit of society.

CHAPTER 6

Conclusions

This study is not intended to be a biography of Enrico Mattei, although it must be admitted that the very nature of its subject matter has made it almost impossible to avoid biographical overtones. Mattei would be a fascinating subject for a biographer. My objective has been to examine an unusual phenomenon in power in which Mattei happens to have played a major role. While Mattei lived it was extremely difficult to avoid giving primary attention to the author, producer, and star of the ENI Group. Mattei's influence is still strong and will remain so for many years.

THE MAN MATTEI

This was a controversial man, and controversy was present even in his tragic end. Neither the Italian nor the foreign press has wholly accepted accidental means as the cause of Mattei's death. The crash in the fog has been attributed to sabotage and even to suicide. Some have said that the crash was further evidence of Mattei's remarkable luck. He died a hero and received a state funeral from his country at a time when storm clouds were gathering over him, over his record, and his reputation, when a few more months or a year might have changed the course of history. There is no question that trouble lay ahead for Enrico Mattei. Yet he had been through troubled episodes before and had emerged each time in a stronger position. I do not believe that anyone could have predicted with much assurance that Mattei would soon have been heading into a decline. No matter what happens to ENI and to Italy in the years to come, it always will be possible to say that things would have been better, or at the least different, if Enrico Mattei had lived.

History will record that Mattei rose from humble origins to become "the most important individual in Italy." [1] The fact that he presided at Italy's triumph over her stultifying shortages of energy will long be remembered; and Italians will not soon forget the economic "miracle" that occurred during Mattei's rise to power. Although hindsight and the passage of time will disclose more and more of Mattei's defects and errors of act and judgment, it will become increasingly difficult to establish clear-cut chains of cause and effect. The depreciating evidence, whatever it may be, will not easily overcome the weight of the Po gas, the spectacular resurrection of Ravenna, the lower prices of gasoline and fertilizer, and the new pride and confidence which Mattei gave to Italy. Even if we could prove that the material achievements attributed to Mattei were not deserved, the intangibles of attitude and spirit that Mattei stimulated in Italy would long remain to his credit.

There is strong evidence that in the months before his death Mattei had recognized two of the traps into which his past conduct and motives had led him, and had taken steps to extricate himself. In the long run the most important of these was Mattei's assumption that the Fanfani government's "opening to the left" would work to the benefit of ENI. On the basis of this assumption, Mattei became one of Fanfani's strongest supporters in the fight to lure the Nenni Socialists away from the Communists. When the "opening" became a fact and the socialist wing of the Christian Democratic Party began to make clear what this meant in terms of governmental policies, Mattei shifted his support to the more moderate factions in the party. He finally realized that socialist ideology does not leave much room for an independent state company like ENI, and that a stronger government meant more interference, more control, and a weaker ENI. Mattei's shift may have occurred in time to save some of ENI's prerogatives. Some of the Socialists in the Christian Democratic Party will resist the bureaucratizing of ENI and IRI, and a few who welcomed ENI's political drive, its contacts with the USSR (in the face of American protests), and its penetration of African markets, will fight to retain some of ENI's independence. ENI probably will never return to the pinnacle of independence it enjoyed under Mattei, but it may be able to achieve equilibrium somewhere between that level and the level of "a gutless state enterprise like the old IRI." [2]

The second major trap from which Mattei may have tried to free himself was the trap created jointly by ENI's shortage of crude oil and the Russian oil contract. As pointed out in other parts of this study, finding "big oil" was almost essential if Mattei and ENI were to stay out of the clutches of the Russians. The Russian contract does not expire until 1965 and is renewable, but if ENI does not find oil in large quantities by 1965, the renewal may be at less favorable terms dictated by the USSR. The problem may have to be faced earlier than 1965, inasmuch as the quantities obtainable under the current contract decline rapidly after 1963. Short of finding "big oil" immediately, the only obvious escape is to make peace with the international oil fraternity and obtain a supply from them. After a long history of friction, this would not have been easy for Mattei, but there are some indications that such peacemaking was underway at the time of his death. There were rumors [3] that Mattei had made a deal with Jersey Standard and that he not only had settled the long-standing court battle over their jointly owned Bari refinery but had also worked out a sale of Esso crude to ENI at prices favorable enough to eliminate the Russians from contention. Whether the ENI-Esso contract made public in 1963 is the one which Mattei was rumored to have negotiated is not known. What is known about the ENI-Esso contract suggests that the supply of crude oil thus provided to ENI will be in addition to, and not in place of, the Russian oil. It would appear that renegotiation of the contract with the USSR will be necessary unless ENI immediately develops substantial sources of its own. Mattei's successors may have more difficulty than did he in obtaining attractive terms and selling the Russian oil contract in Italy.[4]

Even if Mattei did in fact make peace with Jersey Standard he did not let that bring to an end his coöperation with the Communists. During 1962 he had completed arrangements for a $200,-000,000 trade deal with Communist China and at the time of his death was working on a plan to link his Mediterranean pipeline system with a Russian line originating in the Urals and terminating on the Danube.[5] Mattei may have mellowed and matured in some respects over the years, but his behavior frequently resulted in serious danger to Italy and to the West and seemed, in 1962, to be getting worse rather than better. His defective knowledge of foreign affairs and his failure to understand or appreciate the risks involved in his machinations made him a very dangerous man to be guiding Italian foreign policy. He seemed to see the cold war as simply an extension of his "antimonopoly" battle in Italy. If anything can destroy the hero's reputation which Mattei has in Italy, it will be the repercussions of some of the foreign policy he influenced. Fortunately for Italy and the West future presidents of ENI probably will never have the freedom that Mattei had to make major foreign policy without the supervision and control of the Italian government. Furthermore, the Common Market countries have agreed that in a few years the international trade policies of the individual states will be controlled by majority vote of the members. Only Italy, among the six EEC countries, has supported a policy of heavy reliance on Eastern-bloc oil, but the pressure of Russian oil on the West is only just now really coming to be felt.

Mattei brought to a vast government empire the ingenuity, originality, and energy commonly associated with private enterprise, but his willful genius often brought more of risk than of benefit. Italy can now accept and appreciate the many benefits brought by Mattei and hope that the risks may be avoided. Although we cannot fail to admire the achievement of this giant among entrepreneurs we must nevertheless concur in the view expressed by C. L. Sulzberger in the *New York Times:* "But it will probably be a good thing for his country to hand the fuel trust to the direction of a man with less genius and more sense of discipline." [6]

THE FUTURE OF ENI

It is obvious that ENI will never be the same without Mattei. So much of ENI's power and influence was personified in him that, even if another strong leader should appear, the situation as it existed between 1953 and 1962 would not be duplicated. The future of ENI rests not so much on the character of its new leaders as it does on two issues over which its new leaders will have little or no control. The first of these issues has to do with the ultimate results of Mattei's decisions and actions in the past. The second issue is whether the Italian government will elect to try to continue Mattei's policies.

Much has been said in this study about the possible future effects of Mattei's actions. Only a few comments need be added here. The heavy burden of long-term debt carried by ENI may prove to be a source of serious difficulties for ENI, for its multitude of operating companies and for the Italian government. Although one cannot safely apply to a state company the same financial criteria that would be applicable to a private company, some of these criteria do have relevance, both economic and political, to the stability and prospects of even a state-owned firm—especially to a company with the freedom and independence enjoyed by ENI. Undervalued assets and unreported income provide a small element of safety but not enough to mitigate ENI's pressing need to increase its sales and income to the point where the debt can be carried with a minimum of danger. None of ENI's present activities, except the Po gas, give much promise of being able to provide the financial improvement that probably is necessary if ENI is to avoid serious repercussions. Like so many of Mattei's actions, the solution to the heavy debt burden was predicated on hitting "big oil." The way of a public company is not easy when it has justified its existence, at least in part, on its ability to operate with little or no profit, and then must incur an oppressive long-term debt in order to finance its operations. The finances of a government bureau are a part of the national budget, and a private company need not be embarrassed by a comfortable margin of gross profit. But ENI is neither a government bureau nor a private company and is further encumbered by public relations commitments made on its behalf by Mattei in the past.

Mattei's policy of low cost or politically motivated oil concessions may also prove to be ENI's undoing. In a situation where finding "big oil" probably was ENI's single most important need, it was foolhardy to base concession decisions on anything except maximum probability of success. The Russian oil contract did not supply enough of a hedge because it is likely that much of the Russian oil had to go into no-profit gasoline and because the success of the deal with the USSR was also dependent, in part, on ENI's finding "big oil" and not having to renew the contract. A deal with one of the major international oil companies on favorable terms may give ENI another breathing spell, but probably no one in either ENI or the government would be happy with ENI's being reduced permanently to the status of an oil dealer rather than an oil producer, and even this change in policy probably would not alleviate the financial problem.

The decision which the government now must make is especially complicated because it contains two facets, the solutions to which are essentially self-contradictory. The preservation of ENI as an economic power may conflict with the continuation of ENI as a political force. Mattei was able to wear both uniforms for reasons of personality, history, and political association which were peculiar to himself. There appears to be no one on the Italian scene who can duplicate his unusual combination of characteristics. For example, much of Mattei's power depended upon his ability to obtain and keep the support of the far left. He accomplished this, to a great extent, by his attacks on private business and on the "foreign monopolists," but he continued to behave very much like the people he so vigorously assailed. The strong candidates for Mattei's post are much more closely identified with the private sectors of the Italian economy and really cannot be expected to solicit or obtain far-left support. The more leftist candidates for the job may be able to get the leftist political support but seem unlikely to be able to maintain ENI as an economic force. The government's problem is further complicated by the fact that it must make another similar appointment for the recently nationalized electrical industry (ENEL).[7] A new "super-energy agency" is a possibility, but not a very likely one, and would not answer the basic question as to what these state enterprises can or should be.

The weight of the evidence would seem to indicate a much weaker ENI in the years to come and a much higher level of government intervention in the activities of the Ente. This result will come about no matter what decision the government makes. The decision of the government will influence only the degree and the speed with which the result will appear.

LESSONS TO BE LEARNED

This study is more than a history and a prognostication. Mattei and ENI are more than interesting phenomena. We are intrigued by ENI's future and by the role it, and other state enterprises, will play in Italy, but there is a great deal about the ENI experience in Italy that can be of use to us in a broader environment. Much of ENI's wider significance is within the scope of power analysis, already has been considered in detail in Chapter 5, and will be referred to only collaterally here. In addition to power theory, however, there are several other areas in which conclusions may be suggested and lessons may be learned from the rich and varied experience which ENI has provided. These conclusions and lessons can be summarized in two simple statements: (1) Whether a great industrial organization is public or private and whether it is of one legal form or another are relatively unimportant in analyzing many of its economic, political, and social characteristics. (2) The public corporation and the mixed economy may provide a tenable "third way" for those new or underdeveloped countries which find neither capitalism nor socialism wholly adaptable to their needs. Statement (1) will be considered here, and statement (2) will be examined in the concluding section of this chapter.

Before attacking these broader issues, however, let one brief comment be made with regard to the accountability of public corporations. Other portions of this study have devoted space to the subject of accountability, but it is not giving too much weight to this important topic to refer to it again in conclusion. A prominent factor in Mattei's ability to rise to pre-eminence in Italy's political and economic scene was the lack of any effective auditing procedures with regard to ENI. The absence of a genuine audit made it possible for Mattei to do things which could not otherwise have been done, as we already have seen, and protected him from governmental supervision and control. Attacks on Mattei from any quarter were, necessarily, based on rumor and conjecture. Members of Parliament found it impossible to obtain any facts on which defensible criticisms of Mattei and ENI could be based. Ministers who tried to exert influence over Mattei or his policies discovered that they could not obtain accurate information on which to build a policy or an order. Every attempt to get information or to exercise control over Mattei was quickly shifted to the broad arena of public relations, where Mattei was supreme. The fact that much good came from Mattei's highhanded and autocratic behavior is not an argument against an effective and independent audit of state enterprise. If the useful and powerful tool of the public corporation is to be widely employed, machinery to assure valid and effective auditing procedures in an indispensable part of the system.[8] The dangers of domination of the state by irresponsible state enterprise are too great to be outweighed by any conceivable benefits that might be obtained. Mattei and ENI will long be the paramount examples of the truth of this simple doctrine.

In spite of a strong predilection for seeing contrasts between public and private enterprise, between socialist and capitalist economies, and between Italy and the United States, I was struck by the large number of similarities and parallels that characterize certain aspects of these comparisons. It was not that the differences were so few but that the similarities were so many and, in some areas, so important. A study in power is not the proper place to examine in detail these other phenomena, but these phenomena do play an important peripheral role in the environment of power and tend to support, to some extent, the argument for a generalized concept of power.

The policies of the Italian government with regard to private economic power and exploitation have been based, especially since World War II, on a program of direct government intervention through outright nationalization or other comparable means. Heavy concentrations of private power have been met with even heavier concentrations of power in the hands of various forms of state enterprise. In many cases, the control over the state enterprise by the popularly responsible portions of the government has been such that abuses of the power were fewer and less extensive than had been the case when the power was in private hands. In other cases, however, and ENI under Mattei is the best example, the same problems of power which brought about government intervention continued as before, or were aggravated or were replaced by other serious problems. It has been persuasively argued that politics, in the broader sense, is autonomous, and that the problems of power are essentially the same in a socialist as in a capitalist economy, in a publicly as in a privately controlled sector of the society, and that the dangers and problems and applications of power are specific to the power being exercised. "Man's political existence develops a specific type of rationality which cannot be reduced to economics," said Paul Ricoeur.[9] Large organizations have many attributes and problems in common, and large economic organizations, whether public or private, appear to have even more.

In terms of important characteristics, there is very little to choose as between a large American corporation whose ownership is so widely held as to be of no significance in the conduct of the affairs of the organization and a large state enterprise like ENI whose control by the government, especially during the Mattei regime, is so nebulous and weak as to be of no great significance either. Just as large American corporations occasionally make the traditional bows in the direction of the shareholder, so does ENI make a traditional gesture in the direction of the Ministry of State Participations and the government, and both managements go on doing much as they please in very much the same way and, oddly enough, for very much the same reasons. From these premises flows the possible conclusion that efforts to end economic exploitation by direct government intervention in the economy, as in Italy, may or may not end economic exploitation in the sector involved and may produce dangers and abuses of their own.

ENI's goals, as expressed by Mattei, and the goals expressed by any large, progressive American private corporation are remarkably similar, especially if we eliminate from consideration some of the more extreme statements about "capitalist exploiters" on one hand and "creeping socialism" on the other. Both purport to follow, and often do follow, long-range policies in which the public interest is of paramount importance. Many of the policies and pronouncements are indistinguishable. Many large American corporations support public education, for example, or advocate changes and improvements at various educational levels; ENI has long played a role in Italian education and has made many recommendations for its improvement. Large American corporations have become concerned with the social and political impacts of their policies and decisions; ENI has a social studies group in its headquarters organization to appraise these same kinds of impacts. There is little evidence to indicate that the decisions or policies arrived at are very much different. Perhaps this result should not be surprising. A. A. Berle and others [10] have been pointing for years at the political nature of the large corporation and at its relative freedom from substantive accountability. It seems only natural that a large public corporation of an obviously political nature and free from effective governmental control should produce similar goals and means for their implementation. In both organizations, one of the fundamental goals, though unexpressed, is that of preserving organizational existence and identity. In the long run, similar goals will tend to produce similar policies and behavior.

In an excellent article Charles R. Dechert has followed much this same line of reasoning. He concludes, however: "Perhaps the major difference between ENI and the huge American or international corporations lies in ENI's politicizing economic activity, its sensitivity to public opinion, and its conscious use of industrial resources to guarantee its autonomy and to influence public opinion and political decision." [11] I suggest that these "differences" are really more variations among the major confirmations of similarity and are differences only in degree. What large American corporation does not politicize economic activity, is not sensitive to public opinion, and does not use its industrial resources to guarantee its autonomy and to influence public opinion and political decision? These are exactly the things which a large economic organization, public or private, operating without effective accountability, does do.

The history of the development of American corporate society has been one of interaction and reaction between and among the economic, political, and social spheres of our society. Though over a shorter period of time and along a somewhat different track, the same has been true of the development of the Italian "economic public corporations." In the United States, the political reaction to abuses of economic power in private hands was the antitrust laws, whose basic premise was the preservation of a competitive economic system. In Italy, the reaction to the same stimulus was direct government intervention in the offending sector of the economy, often taking the form of outright nationalization, the underlying philosophy of which obviously was quite different from that in the United States. The problems of industrial society were not to be this easily solved, however, and counterreactions were the next step in the evolutionary development. It soon was clear in the United States that a competitive economy made up of relatively small units was probably not best suited to keeping up with the burgeoning technology, population, and markets that accompanied the transition to an industrial society; the result was an economy characterized by a few very large-scale private organizations operating under oligopolistic conditions. It became evident in Italy that the spineless government bureau and the weak, politically dominated state enterprise could not cope with the problems of modern industrial society; the result was the large public corporation which, under a strong and aggressive leader and a minimum of government control, could develop the attributes necessary to meet the conditions. Because the conditions were similar, the institutions evolved to meet them also were similar.

ENI has demonstrated, a generation or more later, many of the same growth characteristics that accompanied the development of large private corporations in the United States and elsewhere. The aggressive, creative, iconoclastic, and egoistic personality seems to dominate the early phases but is later replaced by professional managers of a more conservative and coöperative nature. Some of the organizations never survive the transition, as ENI may not, whereas others go on to become important and lasting features of the society, as has been the case with so many large corporations in the United States. The fact that ENI is government-owned appears not to be the key factor in its evolution. The mixed Italian system of a few large private economic organizations and a few large public economic organizations may prove to be as effective a solution to the problems of industrial society as the American system of large private corporations and, for Italy, perhaps superior.

It has been suggested [12] that if creative personalities could be carefully selected and placed in command of state enterprises, instead of leaving such selections to chance, society might have at its bidding a useful economic and political tool. The problems of making the selection and the risks involved should the wrong criteria be employed do not augur well for this alternative. Chance will still control, and the problems will continue to be those of walking the narrow line between ineffective operation on one hand and abuses of power on the other.

It is possible that ENI has been a unique phenomenon generated by unique circumstances and that there is nothing in the ENI experience that can be of use or application elsewhere. The evidence seems to point in the opposite direction, however, and the parallels outlined above suggest that ENI cannot be removed from the mainstream of organizational behavior, no matter how unique the ENI episode may have been. In the final section of this chapter, we examine still another way in which this study of ENI may prove its ultimate worth.

THE PUBLIC CORPORATION—A THIRD FORM?

An additional facet of the ENI phenomenon deserves brief mention before we bring our account to a close. The public corporation, as a means of achieving common economic, social and political goals, has had to take a back seat in our discussion of ENI and Mattei. It was forced there by Mattei's total domination of the scene and by the fact that it is extremely difficult in the case of ENI to separate the form of organization from the man who so completely overshadowed it. But ENI and the other Italian public corporations are more than just a background for the saga of Mattei. They also play a part in the broader and much more fundamental problems of modern industrial society.

Man's efforts to meet and solve the problems of industrial society have taken several forms. A. A. Berle has said that the large business corporation in the United States and the socialist commissariat in the USSR are the two most successful forms yet devised to deal with these problems,[18] but no one has suggested that either of the forms is the best that can be created or the last that will be employed. The problems of modern industrial society have not all been solved and there is no reason to believe that man's attempts to solve them will cease. Actually, a third form which had its origins in the period between the two World Wars had considerable use after the Second World War, especially in Europe, and shows signs of having enough organizational, ideological, and economic potential to enable it to occupy the vast, disputed territory between the other two.

This third form, the modern public corporation, appears to enjoy several advantages over the other two forms. Most important among them is the strong possibility that it may provide a powerful ideological attraction in many of the new nations and in most of the underdeveloped older nations that now are torn between the extremes of free enterprise capitalism, which they are not advanced enough to employ, and the monolithic Communist state, which they would just as soon avoid if possible. The predicament of these nations is difficult for us in the ad-

vanced industrial societies to understand. Where we had generations of relatively slow evolutionary development to carry us
from local markets, small-scale production, and simple technology into our present mass markets, large-scale production, and
fantastic technology, many of the new and underdeveloped
nations are trying to make the transition into modern industrial
society from no markets, no production, and no technology, in
the modern sense, and to do it in the span of a few short years.
Where we had social, religious, and cultural attitudes and institutions admirably adapted for industrial society, many other
nations must now build hastily on foundations little removed
from the Stone Age. Confronted with unpalatable or impossible
alternatives far too sophisticated and advanced for their circumstances or distasteful in terms of the political commitments involved, most of these countries lean dangerously close to the
latter in order to get the planning and discipline they so desperately need, and more often than not find themselves unable to
withstand the pressures and blandishments of the Communist
left. Important also, as Dechert has said, the public corporation
(or the mixed economy) "appeals to precisely the same nationalistic political elites that are primary Soviet targets." [14]

Under pressure from large and influential numbers of our own
people, who ignorantly persist in equating every deviation from
nineteenth-century enterprise capitalism with the twentieth-
century political Communism of the USSR, our aid to many of
the new and underdeveloped nations has been based on economic,
political, and social assumptions which make sense in an advanced
industrial society but which makes nonsense in Ghana, Mali, or
Laos. We have offered these countries no alternatives other than
our own and have lost or are losing many of them as a result.
Where they have sought to use or to develop other institutions
which may be more consistent with local conditions, they have
received only token aid or encouragement from us.

In our preoccupation with the threat of Communism, we have
overlooked an economic institution which is thoroughly and
completely Western in its origins and much better suited to underdeveloped conditions than is the private business firm. Where the

Communists are forced by their own ideology into a position where they can offer only one alternative, the socialist commissariat and its smothering political side effects, we can avoid letting ourselves be put into the same uncompromising and inflexible position of being able to offer no alternative to the system that works so well for us. The Communists cannot permit the use of the public corporation because to do so presupposes an economy which is essentially private and self-regulatory in character, a supposition completely inconsistent with Communist dogma. On the other hand, the use of the public corporation is consistent with our economic system and with basic principles of freedom and commitment to the rule of law. Though we have used it rarely ourselves, owing to the lack of any pressing need, we have used it very successfully on occasion and should not raise barriers to its encouragement in countries where the need for it is great.

The public corporation is in the Western democratic tradition, and it also presupposes an economy where private enterprise plays an important role. The resulting "mixed economy" will have great attraction for the new and developing countries and will provide them with more alternatives and greater flexibility than does the present all or nothing choice between socialism and capitalism. Most important, perhaps, is its consistency with principles of freedom and individual choice, a consistency which can be maintained with proper institutional safeguards and constant watchfulness.

Apart from the relevance of the public corporation to our program of foreign aid and to the contest with international Communism, there is much of interest in the device as a political, social, and economic phenomenon, comparable in some European countries with the development of the giant modern corporation in the United States. The economy of England, where the modern public corporation was early employed, has been considerably revamped and bolstered in certain sectors largely as a result of this device. Similar results have been obtained in France, and the postwar "Italian Miracle" is in no small part due to the aggressive and innovative performance of ENI. Although in none of these countries can the public corporation yet be called "characteristic" of the economy in the same way that the large modern corporation is characteristic of the American economy, its very presence in the economy, side by side with strictly private corporations, has in a sense become characteristic of the économies of England, France, and especially Italy, as well as of some other European countries. The nature of the modern public corporation is such that the assumption of a dominant economic role would be inconsistent with its purpose and concept.

In his perceptive "Politics of Industry" Walton Hamilton wrote that most of what was daring and ingenious in statecraft had, for the last fifty years, come from the corporation and not from the state.[15] He went on to describe how the corporate device had been used to penetrate political boundaries, to spread modern technology around the world, and to engage in a host of other activities from which the political state is barred. But Hamilton and others, including the author of this paper,[16] have called attention to some of the dangers inherent in a situation where private corporations may compete with the political state in the art of statecraft. Where a corporation supplements the activities of the state or simply enters the vacuum left by the inactive state, its daring and ingenious ventures into statecraft usually can be viewed with admiration. There are many things which the corporation can do which the state cannot, or which the corporation does do which the state does not, or which the corporation can do better. However, where the corporation's ventures into statecraft interfere or conflict with or are inconsistent with proper activities of the state, continued exercises of statecraft by the corporation cannot be tolerated. Each of these areas has been the subject of research, comment, and speculation, but one major related area has received little attention. How can present techniques of statecraft be utilized to permit the national state to exercise or control the exercise of statecraft in areas where the state has an interest but where international barriers and boundaries foreclose its direct participation? The modern public corporation offers a partial answer to this question.

There is little doubt that statecraft needs improvement and modernization. Hydrogen bombs, space exploration, Telstar communications, computers of fantastic sophistication, and 700-miles-per-hour transportation all exist and operate in a political and social world preoccupied with urban squalor, with getting the three princes of Laos under the same roof, and with keeping the new and underdeveloped nations from falling under Communist domination. Perhaps what we have learned from Mattei and ENI can be of help to us in providing new techniques of statecraft and in avoiding the pitfalls and problems that we have just witnessed in Italy. The modern public corporation is not yet fully developed as an instrument of statecraft, but it already contains much promise. If we can develop the device for our own use, where needed, and can commend and guide its use by some of the new and underdeveloped nations of the world, we may be able to count it as a major achievement in our efforts to solve the problems of industrial society. In order to maximize the results obtained with the public corporation and other social, political, and economic institutions, and to minimize the risk of abuse of power, it also will be necessary to continue our endeavors in the realm of understanding and controlling phenomena of power. In this respect, our observations of Mattei and ENI may pay the greatest dividends.

Notes

CHAPTER 1

[1] Montanelli, Indro, in *Corriere della Sera*, Milan, July 13–17, 1962.
[2] The electric power industry was already partly nationalized.
[3] June 20, 1962.
[4] Montanelli, *supra*, note 1.
[5] Organized in 1933.
[6] Il Ministero dell'Industria e del Commercio, *L'Istituto per la Ricostruzione Industriale* (Torino, 1955), in 3 volumes.
[7] Montanelli, *supra*, note 1.
[8] The conduct of *Il Giorno* in 1961 during the attempt of the Communist Deputies to persuade the Sicilian provincial legislature to revoke the Gulf concession at Ragusa is a good example.
[9] Apparently the pipe being delivered to the Russians is fitted with valves manufactured in ENI's Nuovo Pignone plant under license from the owners of the English patents. These valves make it possible to transport several fluids through a pipeline simultaneously. The belief is widespread in Europe that Mattei's pipe is being used by the Russians to build pipelines from their fields to the frontiers of Western Europe. Prime Minister Macmillan's protest to Fanfani over this conduct by an arm of the Italian government came to nothing. (See Montanelli's account of this affair as reported in *Atlas*, September, 1962, p. 206.)
[10] Law of January 11, 1957, n. 6.

CHAPTER 2

[1] To replace Italy's natural gas with imported petroleum would now require 70 to 80 billion lire a year in foreign exchange.

[2] Law of April 3, 1926, n. 556. The Azienda was created under private law with the stock owned by public agencies.

[3] The Partisans demonstrated their anti-fascist attitudes toward the end of World War II and, thus, put themselves in good positions for these appointments, but the fact that so many of them were Communists kept the number chosen rather low. The professors probably had the best opportunity for avoiding active coöperation with Mussolini and entanglements with the Communists, which helps to explain why, in the postwar period, so many government offices and agencies were headed by "professors."

[4] Mattei's primary association was with a Catholic Resistance force (Brigate del Popolo).

[5] The instructions were set forth in a letter from Finance Minister Soleri dated May 15, 1945, but probably were prescribed elsewhere as well.

[6] At one stage, Mattei raised money for drilling in the Po Valley by selling 49 per cent of a small refinery to British Petroleum, but this was after the initial strikes had been made.

[7] One story told in Italy is that Mattei started a rumor that "the enemy," the foreign oil companies, were going to sabotage the gas fields in order to lend credence to their argument that Mattei was incompetent. After the rumor was well established, Mattei organized his ex-Partisans to protect the installations and effectively drew around himself the sacred cloak of the Resistance.

[8] Law of January 11, 1957, n. 6. (The Cortese Law.)

[9] The statute limited the size of the drilling area granted to any one company on a single permit and limited the total area of authorization by region and in Italy as a whole. If oil or gas were found, the area of exploitation was reduced to a small square or rectangle around the find, and a continuous band one kilometer wide extending all the way around this area was reserved to the state. The Minister for Industry and Commerce was authorized to revoke concessions without compensation, after hearing, on grounds specified in the statute; although the grounds appeared to contemplate more or less serious lapses on the part of the oil companies, the language was not as clear as it might have been. All foreign oil companies left the mainland of Italy after the law was passed.

[10] See Chapter 4.

[11] Such provision has now been made.

[12] Law of February 10, 1953, n. 136.

[13] *Ibid.*, Article 5.

[14] *Ibid.*, Articles 5 and 7.

[15] *Ibid.*, Article 2.

[16] The President of ENI is named by the President of the Council of Ministers. *Ibid.*, Article 12. The term is for three years; Mattei was reappointed in 1957 and 1960.

[17] Participants in the Iran Consortium: British Petroleum (the old Anglo-Iranian)—40 per cent; Royal Dutch-Shell—14 per cent; American Group (Standard of New Jersey, Socony-Vacuum, Gulf, Standard of California, Texas Company—7 per cent each)—35 per cent; Cie Française des Pétroles—6 per cent; 2d American Group (Iricon: Richfield, American Independent, Standard of Ohio, Getty, Signal, Atlantic, Hancock, Tidewater, San Jacinto)—5 per cent.

[18] Montanelli, Indro, in *Corriere della Sera*, Milan, July 13, 1962.

[19] The Arabian Oil Company.

[20] Jersey Standard is alleged to have refused to refine the Egyptian oil in the ESSO-ENI jointly owned refineries, but Mattei's threat to have the ESSO interest nationalized supposedly led to a change of policy by ESSO.

[21] See Chapter 4.

[22] In Cyrenaica; but at least twelve other oil companies also have concessions in Libya.

[23] See Chapter 4.

[24] ENI's consolidated balance sheet for April 30, 1962, shows assets of approximately $1.2 billion; Mattei, in the summer of 1962, said $1.6 billion; most experts suggest a figure more like $2 billion.

[25] Actually, ENI was engaged in limited Egyptian activities as early as 1955, but these did not become significant until a year or two later.

[26] See Chapter 3.

[27] Law of February 10, 1953, n. 136, Article 1.

[28] Some of these activities were inherited with the original combination of companies in 1953. A few of this type have been disposed of, as is discussed in Chapter 3.

CHAPTER 3

[1] For one version of this story, see Montanelli, Indro, in *Corriere della Sera*, Milan, July 13–17, 1962: summarized in *Atlas*, September, 1962, p. 207.

[2] Mattei's answer to Montanelli's charges appeared in *Corriere della Sera* and also in *Atlas*. See *Atlas*, October, 1962, p. 296.

[3] The value of the lira in relation to the dollar has remained substantially unchanged since 1953. Consequently, adjustments for cyclical changes are not necessary.

[4] This figure is the amount of the original state subsidy and is a gross

undervaluation. Estimates of the actual value of the assets handed over to ENI in 1953 run to five or six times this amount. Consolidated assets of the Group were undervalued in about the same proportion.

[5] Unless otherwise indicated, financial data come from ENI's own reports. ENI's financial year ends on April 30; if not specified, financial data will be as of April 30 of the year mentioned.

[6] Note that ENI's production of liquid petroleum in Italy in 1961 was well below the level of 1960.

[7] The information in this paragraph came from ENI's annual reports.

[8] *Il Giorno* is not mentioned anywhere in the ENI reports.

[9] Mattei's answer to Montanelli. See *Atlas*, October, 1962, p. 295.

[10] ENI, *Energy and Hydrocarbons in 1960* (Rome, 1961), p. 192.

[11] These data were gathered from a number of sources, including some of ENI's own publications.

[12] See *Atlas*, October, 1962, pp. 293–297. Mattei died October 28 of that year.

[13] Letter quoted by Montanelli in *Atlas*, September, 1962, pp. 207–208.

[14] ENI, Annual Report, April 30, 1961, p. 90.

[15] The Italian Government, through IRI, has a 7.3 per cent participation in Montecatini.

[16] ENI, Annual Report, April 30, 1961, p. 90.

[17] Mattei, *supra*, note 2.

[18] ENI, *supra*, note 16, p. 91.

[19] The Ministry of State Participations very early abandoned its efforts to employ outside experts for investment program planning. *Giornale degli Economisti*, Jan.–Feb., 1959, vol. 18, pp. 5–6.

CHAPTER 4

[1] "Natural vapors" refers to the development of power from natural steam sources. These are of minor importance in the total ENI picture.

[2] Ministry of State Participations, *Policy and Program Report* (Rome, 1961), pp. 3–4.

[3] After Mattei's death in October, 1962, Ingegnere Girotti was given the title of Direttore Generale in order to denote his assuming primary responsibilities for actual operations. Prior to Mattei's death Girotti was referred to as Vice-Direttore Generale. Theoretically, Mattei was both Presidente and Direttore Generale, but did not use the latter title.

See Chapter 5 for a more detailed discussion of the changes in organization and personnel that followed Mattei's death.

[4] Details of the organization of the company and the duties of its officers and boards are found in the Law of February 10, 1953, and in the Charter, decreed by the President of the Republic, December 22, 1954, n. 1523.

[5] Law of February 10, 1953, n. 136, Article 8.

[6] *Ibid.*

[7] *Ibid.*, Article 22.

[8] The statute establishing the Ministry of State Participations conveys the impression that state companies are expected to show a profit or, perhaps, not to show losses; but there is no guidance in the statute and no policy in the Ministry as to how this criterion of performance is to be established or measured.

[9] Resolutions of the High Economic Council of the Arab League, January 21–26, 1956, included the following: "Future concessions should contain a stipulation forbidding foreign governments to own stock in the concessionary companies." This resolution was adopted May 25–June 3, 1957.

[10] For further details on concession agreements, see: Lenczowski, George, *Oil and State in the Middle East* (Ithaca: 1960); Finnie, David H., *Desert Enterprise* (Cambridge, 1958); and Fanning, Leonard M., *Foreign Oil and the Free World* (New York, 1954).

[11] Société Irano-Italienne des Pétroles (SIRIP).

[12] Montanelli used this phrase in his series of articles in *Corriere della Sera*, July 13–17, 1962.

[13] Tumiati, *The Financial Times* (London), July 13, 1960, p. 1.

[14] By actual count, the number of pages in *Stampa e Oro Nero* decreased from 1656 in 1958, to 1513 in 1959 and to 1075 in 1960.

[15] *Atlas*, September, 1962, p. 194. *Il Giorno* said not a word about Montanelli's articles or Mattei's reply.

[16] *Corriere della Sera* and *24 Ore* took Gulf's side in this dispute.

[17] Mattei provided the Russians with their first important breakthrough in their international oil offensive and they dealt with him as though he were a chief of state.

[18] During the Gulf-Ragusa controversy in 1961, it was revealed that Gulf paid Sicily a 12.5 per cent royalty on the production of its Ragusa field, while ENI paid a 4 per cent royalty at Gela. *Il Giorno* explained this discrepancy by calling attention to the low quality of the Gela crude.

[19] ENI, *Annual Report and Statement of Accounts*, April 30, 1961, p. 85.

[20] AGIP, "Oil Exploration in Italy," Report of December 18, 1945, p. 97.

[21] Reply to Montanelli, in *Atlas*, October, 1962, p. 296.

[22] *Il Giorno*, October 7, 1961.

[23] Reported in *Atlas*, September, 1962, pp. 199–200.

[24] *Atlas*, October, 1962, p. 295.

[25] *Ibid.*, p. 296.

CHAPTER 5

[1] See Sorokin, Pitirim A., and Walter A. Lunden, *Power and Morality* (Boston, Porter Sargent, 1959).

[2] Cooperman, David, and E. V. Walter, *Power and Civilization* (New York, Thomas Y. Crowell Co., 1962), p. 2.

[3] Coser, Lewis A., and Bernard Rosenberg, *Sociological Theory* (New York, The Macmillan Co., 1957), p. 123.

[4] Goldhamer, Herbert, and Edward A. Shils (eds.), "Types of Power and Status," *The American Journal of Sociology*, 45: 171–172, 1939.

[5] Michels, Roberto, "Authority," *Encyclopedia of the Social Science*, p. 319.

[6] Tawney, Richard Henry, *Equality* (London, G. Allen and Unwin, 1952), pp. 175–176.

[7] D'Antonio, William V., and Howard J. Ehrlich (eds.), *Power and Democracy in America* (Notre Dame, U. of Notre Dame Press, 1961), p. 132.

[8] Gerth, Hans, and C. Wright Mills, *Character and Social Structure* (New York, Harcourt, Brace, 1953), p. 195.

[9] Parsons, Talcott, "The Distribution of Power in American Society," *World Politics*, 10: 140, 1957.

[10] Lasswell, Harold D., and Abraham Kaplan, *Power and Society* (New Haven, Yale University Press, 1950), p. 76.

[11] Ogle, Marbury B., Jr., Louis Schneider and Jay W. Wiley, *Power, Order, and the Economy* (New York, Harper and Brothers, 1954), p. 52.

[12] Parsons, *op. cit.*, p. 140.

[13] Ogle, *op. cit.*, p. 39.

[14] Lasswell, *op. cit.*, p. 10.

[15] Riesman, David, *The Lonely Crowd* (Garden City, Doubleday Anchor, 1959), p. 253.

[16] Early sociological writing on power: Max Weber, Georg Simmel,

and the Italians: Vilfredo Pareto, Roberto Michels, and Gaetano Mosca.

[17] Lasswell, *op cit.*, p. 205.

[18] *Ibid.*, p. 97.

[19] *Ibid.*, p. 94.

[20] Michels, *op. cit.*, p. 319.

[21] Hillenbrand, Martin J., *Power and Morals* (New York, Columbia University Press, 1959), p. 6.

[22] *Ibid.*, p. 45.

[23] Spitz, David, *Democracy and the Challenge of Power* (New York, Columbia University Press, 1958), p. 18.

[24] Mack Smith, Denis, *Italy, A Modern History* (Ann Arbor, University of Michigan Press, 1959), p. 416.

[25] Sterling, Claire, "Mattei, the Condottiere," *Reporter*, April 20, 1958, pp. 20–23.

[26] Law of February 10, 1953, n. 136, Article 15.

[27] Law of December 22, 1956, n. 1589.

[28] ENI, *Annual Report and Statement of Accounts*, April 30, 1961, p. 91.

[29] Neville, Robert, "Italy's New Caesar," *Harper's Magazine*, March, 1961, pp. 79–85.

[30] See Table 3, Chapter 4.

[31] Russell, Bertrand, *Power, A New Social Analysis* (London, W. W. Norton & Co., 1938).

[32] Weber, Max, *From Max Weber: Essays in Sociology*. Translated by H. Gerth and C. W. Mills. (New York, Oxford University Press, 1946), p. 129.

[33] Lasswell, *op. cit.*, p. 76.

[34] *Ibid.*

CHAPTER 6

[1] Sulzberger, C. L., "Life and Death of an Eminence Grise," *New York Times*, November 5, 1962, p. 8, col. 4 (West Coast edition).

[2] *The Economist*, November 3, 1962, p. 500.

[3] *Time*, November 16, 1962, p. 92; *The Economist, op. cit.*, p. 499.

[4] On November 14, 1963, ENI announced a new six-year oil agreement with the USSR that foresees a total importation of 25 million tons of crude oil, in exchange for which ENI has agreed to send Russia synthetic rubber, plastics, chemical products, machinery, textiles, and equipment for chemical and petroleum plants.

[5] Sulzberger, *supra*, note 1.

[6] Editorial of October 31, 1962.

[7] The creation of the new electricity monopoly raises a number of interesting questions with regard to ENI. Electricity already is being generated by ENI from both petroleum and nuclear sources, and a large thermoelectric plant is now under construction at Gela. The most important source of fuel for generating electricity in Italy is petroleum. Many potential areas of coöperation and conflict between the two great energy monopolies suggest themselves. Furthermore, competition from foreign oil companies may be eliminated if the electricity monopoly decides to purchase its entire petroleum needs from ENI. ENI may be forced to give up its activities in the electrical industry.

[8] See *The Public Corporation*, W. Friedmann, ed. (Toronto, Carswell Co., Ltd., 1954).

[9] *In* Cooperman and Walter, *Power and Civiization* (New York, Thomas Y. Crowell Co., 1957), p. 434.

[10] Berle, Adolf A., *The Twentieth Century Capitalist Revolution* (New York, Harcourt, Brace and Company, 1959); *Power Without Property* (New York, Harcourt, Brace and Company, 1959); *The Corporation in Modern Society*, Edward S. Mason, ed. (Cambridge, Harvard University Press, 1960) and Urwick, Lyndall, *Patterns of Management* (Minneapolis, University of Minnesota Press, 1956).

[11] Dechert, Charles R., "Ente Nazionale Idrocarburi: A State Corporation in a Mixed Economy," *Administrative Science Quarterly*, 7: 322, 347, 1962.

[12] *Ibid.*, p. 348.

[13] Berle, Adolf A., in the Foreword to *The Corporation in Modern Society*, *op. cit.*, n. 9, p. ix.

[14] Dechert, *op. cit.*, p. 348.

[15] Hamilton, Walton, *The Politics of Industry* (New York, Alfred A. Knopf, 1957), p. 136.

[16] Votaw, Dow, "The Politics of a Changing Corporate Society," *California Management Review*, Vol. 3, No. 3, 1961.

Index

Lightning Source UK Ltd.
Milton Keynes UK
UKHW012056011021
391518UK00001B/65